Shakespeare's Revision
of *King Lear*

PRINCETON ESSAYS
IN LITERATURE

For a complete list of titles in the series
see pages 169 and 170

Shakespeare's Revision
of *King Lear*

STEVEN URKOWITZ

PRINCETON UNIVERSITY PRESS

Copyright © 1980 by Princeton University Press

Published by Princeton University Press, Princeton, New Jersey
In the United Kingdom: Princeton University Press, Guildford, Surrey

All Rights Reserved

Library of Congress Cataloging in Publication Data will be
found on the last printed page of this book

This book has been composed in VIP Baskerville

Clothbound editions of Princeton University Press books
are printed on acid-free paper, and binding materials are
chosen for strength and durability

Printed in the United States of America by Princeton
University Press, Princeton, New Jersey

FOR MY WIFE,
SUSAN

Contents

	Acknowledgments	ix
I.	Current Opinions on the Texts of *King Lear*	3
	The First Quarto	7
	The Second Quarto	11
	The Folio	12
II.	Textual Variants in Dramatic Contexts	16
III.	Textual Variants and Players' Entrances and Exits	35
IV.	Interrupted Exits and the Textual Variants in Act Three, Scene One	56
V.	The Role of Albany in the Quarto and Folio	80
	Act 1, Scene 1 to Act 5, Scene 1	81
	Act 5, Scene 3	103
VI.	Contemporary Bibliographical Theories and Editorial Practices and the Case for Authorial Revision	129
	Abbreviations of Frequently Cited Works	151
	Notes	153
	Index	167

Acknowledgments

This book has taken me several years to write, and during that time I have accumulated many debts of gratitude, which I can acknowledge though not repay. Jerome Taylor, now of the University of Wisconsin, first encouraged me to study drama at the University of Chicago, and Paul D'Andrea, now of the University of Minnesota, invited me to direct my first Renaissance play. David M. Bevington and Mark Ashin of the University of Chicago patiently guided and encouraged the book's halting progress from its ragged early drafts. G. Blakemore Evans of Harvard University and Michael J. Warren of the University of California at Santa Cruz read and reread the manuscript in its final stages, suggesting valuable revisions and corrections in fact, in tone, and in form. The staffs of the Folger Shakespeare Library, the New York Public Library and its Theatre Collection at Lincoln Center, and the Walter Hampden Memorial Library of the Players Club in New York City aided my research, and my editors, Marjorie Sherwood, Carol Orr, and Robert Brown, cheerfully helped me at Princeton University Press. My greatest and dearest obligation is to my wife, Susan, an actress and a scholar in her own right, who insisted upon honesty in my theatrical imagination and in my prose. Whatever virtues are found here I received as gifts; whatever faults I acknowledge as my own, and I beg that the reader forget and forgive.

Shakespeare's Revision
of *King Lear*

Chapter I

Current Opinions on the Texts of *King Lear*

> *Bast.* If the matter were good my Lord, I durst swear it were his: but in respect of that, I would faine thinke it were not.
> *Glou.* It is his.
> *Bast.* It is his hand, my Lord: but I hope his heart is not in the Contents.[1]

There are three texts of *King Lear*. The first, called the First Quarto, appeared in 1608. The second, printed in the First Folio edition of Shakespeare's works, appeared in 1623. The third, the modern version, is a composite made up from the two early texts; it achieved its basic shape in successive editions published during the eighteenth century.

Editors of the modern text base their work on the premise that Shakespeare wrote only a single original draft of *King Lear*, now unfortunately lost, and that the 1608 Quarto and the 1623 Folio both distort the missing original manuscript. Modern editors assume that their own texts more accurately approach the hypothetical lost original than does either of the two early versions. All editions used in schools follow the modern text; all literary analysis is based on the modern text; and practically all theatrical productions are founded on the modern text.

But I argue that in many specific details—of dialogue, stage movement, spectacle, characterization and plot—either of the two early texts is superior to the modern version; that the Folio text represents a careful and dramatically sensitive revision of the Quarto; and that the revision could have been made by no one other than Shakespeare himself.

Four hundred lines of the modern text of *King Lear*, slightly more than 10 percent of the play, appear in only one or the other of the two early versions of the play. The Quarto contains about three hundred lines not in the Folio, and the Folio contains approximately one hundred lines not found in the Quarto. In addition, at least a thousand isolated words are changed in the two early texts, the punctuation is throughout radically different in style, and about half of the verse lines in the Folio are either printed as prose or differently divided in the Quarto.

One theory after another has been offered to account for the differences between the two early texts. Several of the most important have been proposed intermittently for over two hundred years, each time prompting the same series of objections, opposing theories, and modifications. A reliable determination of the sources of the variants in the early texts of *Lear* has been an elusive goal. Viewing the results of the search for reasonable, or even possible, causes of the variants, the foremost authority in the field concludes: "The truth is that critics have been speculating without proper regard to the probabilities of the case. . . . It is to be feared that a consideration of the various theories so far advanced can only lead to the conclusion that it remains as true today as it was twenty-five years ago that *King Lear* still offers a problem for investigation."[3]

The modern text of *King Lear* follows what is commonly thought to be an acceptable editorial policy. Given its basic form by Theobald in 1733, the modern text was at first based on the unproven assumption that a combination or conflation of lines from both early texts would approximate a hypothetical "original." Some contemporary editors and textual critics, including Alice Walker and G. Blakemore Evans, still maintain this position. Other editors, who perhaps question or even reject the idea of a single authorial original existing prior to the Quarto and the Folio, nevertheless reproduce the text that has become conventionally acceptable. Charles Knight, a practical and successful nineteenth-century editor and publisher, was one of the first to articulate his reasons for adopting the composite text after rejecting its theoretical justification:

more than 10 percent of the play, appear in only one or the other of the two early versions of the play. The Quarto contains about three hundred lines not in the Folio, and the Folio contains approximately one hundred lines not found in the Quarto.[2] In addition, at least a thousand isolated words are changed in the two early texts, the punctuation is throughout radically different in style, and about half of the verse lines in the Folio are either printed as prose or differently divided in the Quarto.

One theory after another has been offered to account for the differences between the two early texts. Several of the most important have been proposed intermittently for over two hundred years, each time prompting the same series of objections, opposing theories, and modifications. A reliable determination of the sources of the variants in the early texts of *Lear* has been an elusive goal. Viewing the results of the search for reasonable, or even possible, causes of the variants, the foremost authority in the field concludes: "The truth is that critics have been speculating without proper regard to the probabilities of the case.... It is to be feared that a consideration of the various theories so far advanced can only lead to the conclusion that it remains as true today as it was twenty-five years ago that *King Lear* still offers a problem for investigation."[3]

The modern text of *King Lear* follows what is commonly thought to be an acceptable editorial policy. Given its basic form by Theobald in 1733, the modern text was at first based on the unproven assumption that a combination or conflation of lines from both early texts would approximate a hypothetical "original." Some contemporary editors and textual critics, including Alice Walker and G. Blakemore Evans, still maintain this position. Other editors, who perhaps question or even reject the idea of a single authorial original existing prior to the Quarto and the Folio, nevertheless reproduce the text that has become conventionally acceptable. Charles Knight, a practical and successful nineteenth-century editor and publisher, was one of the first to articulate his reasons for adopting the composite text after rejecting its theoretical justification:

CHAPTER I

Current Opinions on the Texts of *King Lear*

Bast. If the matter were good my Lord, I durst swear it were his: but in respect of that, I would faine thinke it were not.
Glou. It is his.
Bast. It is his hand, my Lord: but I hope his heart is not in the Contents.[1]

There are three texts of *King Lear*. The first, called the First Quarto, appeared in 1608. The second, printed in the First Folio edition of Shakespeare's works, appeared in 1623. The third, the modern version, is a composite made up from the two early texts; it achieved its basic shape in successive editions published during the eighteenth century.

Editors of the modern text base their work on the premise that Shakespeare wrote only a single original draft of *King Lear*, now unfortunately lost, and that the 1608 Quarto and the 1623 Folio both distort the missing original manuscript. Modern editors assume that their own texts more accurately approach the hypothetical lost original than does either of the two early versions. All editions used in schools follow the modern text; all literary analysis is based on the modern text; and practically all theatrical productions are founded on the modern text.

But I argue that in many specific details—of dialogue, stage movement, spectacle, characterization and plot—either of the two early texts is superior to the modern version; that the Folio text represents a careful and dramatically sensitive revision of the Quarto; and that the revision could have been made by no one other than Shakespeare himself.

Four hundred lines of the modern text of *King Lear*, slightly

> There are passages, indeed, which the [modern] editors have restored from the quartos; and we admit the importance of preserving those passages, upon the principle that not a line which appears to have been written by Shakespeare ought to be lost.... Our copy is literally that of the folio, except that where a passage occurs in the quartos which is not in the folio, we introduce such a passage, printing it, however, in brackets.[4]

With or without brackets, modern editions uniformly present a text of *King Lear* containing all the lines that may be practicably included from the Quarto and the Folio, in an attempt to preserve all of Shakespeare's writing.

The modern composite text of *Lear* is the product of methods first developed for solving classical and Biblical textual problems. Many early writings come down to us in different surviving versions, each ultimately derived from a single lost original; when all variants in alternative texts of a work are introduced by copyists or, in the case of printed books, by compositors, then the recovery of the author's original intentions is frequently possible. Unauthorized changes in individual words, word order, punctuation, lineation, scansion, etc., may be recognized and the original readings recovered in a relatively straightforward manner. These satisfying restorations account for the appeal of bibliographic studies, and upon such work stands the justifiably strong reputation of textual scholarship. But these methods do not work if they are applied to alternative texts created by a revising author.

After more than two hundred years of editorial practices that have led to a text of *King Lear* generally accepted by readers, performers, and scholars, recent scholarship has begun to question even the most basic tenets of conventional editing when they are applied to Shakespearean texts. Arguments which have assumed that Biblical or classical scholarship offered simple analogies to Elizabethan bibliographical problems now appear to contain many contradictions in both theory and fact. Fredson Bowers, after examining the complexities in the current state of Shakespearean textual studies, comments on the basic presumptions behind many established editorial practices: "I submit that the evidence on which we have all grounded certain articles of faith is in reality rather uncertain."[5] Many independent lines of inquiry seem to confirm that Bowers is correct in his basic scepticism. Practically all the assertions that have been made, about the genesis of major variants amounting to many lines each and minor changes in single words or phrases, may have to be reexamined and reevaluated.

Inadvertently, the very success of bibliographic scholarship has limited discussion of the variants of *King Lear* to a small group of highly specialized textual scholars. Until quite recently, this narrow focus seems to have prevented or discouraged other scholars from analyzing literary or dramatic merits of variants in *King Lear*. However, during a fundamental revision of textual theories there is a critical need for cooperation among the various specialists. Phillip Gaskell, author of an important new introduction to bibliography, warns, "Literary judgement alone, without the discipline of textual bibliography, will result in the production of misleading and inaccurate texts as surely as will the mechanical application of bibliographic rules. Textual bibliography is based on the union of literary judgement with bibliographical expertise."[6] For about the first two hundred years, textual study of *King Lear* was overwhelmingly literary in its biases. For the past twenty or thirty years, we have seen predominantly bibliographic analysis. The present study attempts to deal with some of the major problems in the text of *King Lear* in what is hoped to be a useful fusion of these different techniques.

A history of critical opinion on the text of *King Lear* could be a volume in itself. Now, however, although critics maintain considerable differences in particular details, they generally agree that the Quarto text is drawn in some way from Shakespeare's foul papers and the Folio text is derived in some way from a playhouse promptbook used by Shakespeare's company. Critics disagree on why there are differences between the Quarto and Folio, and on which text to follow in specific instances.

The First Quarto

Until the 1950s, most critics subscribed to the theory that the Quarto text was printed from a shorthand report made in the theater by an unauthorized "pirate." First proposed by Lewis Theobald in 1733, this theory was improved and embellished over the years, reaching what is perhaps its most vivid formulation in 1880, when Alexander Schmidt described the following as the probable method by which a disreputable printer acquired his copy:

> It could not have been difficult, where neither pains nor cost were spared, to procure by copyists in the Theatre a passable, nay, even a complete and correct printer's copy. If it proved too much for one shorthand writer, two or three could accomplish it, by relieving each other; and if it could not be finished at the first performance, it could certainly be done at the second or third.[7]

The appeal of this scheme, and of others like it, is that it gives support to the image of Shakespeare as a classical author whose originally flawless writings were soiled and distorted by intervening agents. The shorthand-report theory for the Quarto text of *King Lear* allows critics to ascribe many of its variant readings to what they propose were the "errors" made by the actors in performance, by the acting company during the preparation of the author's text for the stage, by a scribe copying out the actors' parts or the promptbook, by the shorthand reporter when he was in the theater or when he was transcribing his notes, and by the compositor in the printing house.

But two separate developments in textual and theatrical criticism led to the abandonment of both the shorthand-report theory and related theories which assumed that the Quarto was at some point in its history derived from a performing version of the play. First, after decades of debate, it has been conclusively proven and universally accepted that no technique of stenography known in England in 1608 was capable of transcribing anything as difficult as a play.[8] Second, textual critics have realized that the exigencies of producing a large and constantly changing repertory of plays would make revisions of the type found between the Quarto and Folio of *King Lear* highly impractical once either version had been brought to the stage. W. W. Greg, who had been one of the strongest proponents of the reporter theory, later recognized that "had there been a report of a stage performance it would almost certainly have given us a garbled version of F rather than anything resembling Q." He added, "In every respect the quarto text is unsuited to representation."[9] G. I. Duthie argued that actors rather than reporters assembled the Quarto text out of their faulty memories of the parts. His theory was so cumbersome and improbable he withdrew it and confirmed that "Q1, then, does not look like an actors' reconstruction, and my 1949 theory had better be abandoned."[10] Since the Quarto could not have been derived from a performing script or from some recollection of a performance, critics have turned again to examine the possibilities that the Quarto represents a version of *King Lear* made prior to the playhouse promptbook.

Only two theories are now seriously considered as possible explanations for the derivation of the Quarto. The most frequently quoted, though not widely accepted, is Alice Walker's proposal that the Quarto is printed from a surreptitiously made copy of Shakespeare's foul papers.[11] The many flaws in the Quarto, such as misspellings, mislineation of verse, the printing of verse as prose, etc., previously thought of as reporters' errors, are seen by Walker as the results of a hurried and inaccurate transcription made by two boy-actors. They worked, she explains, in the playhouse, one dictating and the other writing. To account for many of the variants in single words and phrases, Walker proposes that the boys unconsciously substituted those "vulgar" or unpoetic variants which appear in the Quarto in the place of the apt and "genuinely Shakespearean" expressions found in the Folio. In order to explain particularly corrupt passages, Walker also argues that the boys often allowed their memories to trick them during the process of transcription; that instead of following their copy when they transcribed scenes in which they had acted, they relied on their faulty recollection of performances rather than on the text before them; that they interpolated words or lines from other scenes or from other passages of dialogue, sometimes getting a syllable or a sound wrong, and sometimes losing or adding an entire line or speech; that, once sold to a printer, their frequently illegible rough copy led the compositor in the printing house to make more errors, and the compositor himself was responsible for still more accidental omissions, inversions, and substitutions.

Despite its many errors and "oddities," Walker argues, "the quarto text is much closer to the foul papers than is widely supposed" (p. 69). (This was written in 1954, when the Quarto was still considered by many editors and textual critics to be a report of a performance.) Walker concludes that the Quarto "is very good text and we shall lose much of the linguistic and dramatic subtlety of *Lear* if the most is not made of the quarto readings" (p. 67).

The unstated premise of Walker's argument is that Shakespeare himself composed nothing but the foul-paper manuscript he turned over to the players. *All* subsequent changes were made by other hands, Walker believes. Michael J. Warren has recently questioned the validity of this premise, the basis not only of Walker's hypothesis but also of all modern composite texts. He points out, first, that there is no real evidence to indicate the existence of a lost "original" antecedent to the Quarto and Folio. And, second, he argues that there is no reason to believe that other hands, not Shakespeare's, created all the alterations from the imagined "original."[12]

The second major theory on the derivation of the Quarto text also holds that it was derived from Shakespeare's foul papers, but the irregularities in the Quarto, according to this theory, reflect the confusions in the foul-paper manuscript itself.

R.W.B. McKerrow proposes that the general class of popular drama printed in quartos, including *King Lear*, contains much more textual confusion than is found in other printed material of the period, not because plays were frequently "pirated," but because "whereas in the case of most book-copy of the time the operation of the licencing laws brought it about that the compositors had a careful fair-copy to work from, in that of the plays they were far more likely to be furnished with an author's rough draft much corrected and never put in order for the press."[13] The fair copy of a play was submitted to the Master of the Revels for censorship. (His endorsement was required "at the latter end of the said booke they doe play.")[14] McKerrow argues that since the fair copy served the double functions of license and promptbook, as a valuable asset the acting company would not release it to a printer if another copy of the play was also available. If the author's working draft was in the possession of the acting company, then that draft rather than the fair-copy promptbook would be given to the printer when the company approved publication. Greg, for one, believes this to be the case at least for the Second Quarto of *Hamlet*, though he rejects this theory for the Quarto of *Lear* because of the magnitude of that text's irregularities (*First Folio*, pp. 316, 378).

Madeleine Doran analyzes the patterns of textual irregularity in the Quarto text, much as Walker does, but she argues that most of the textual irregularity in the Quarto is the result of authorial revision made in the foul-paper manuscript. She proposes that the Quarto's passages of misaligned verse result from new matter being written in the margins of pages, on slips pasted into the text, and on leaves inserted in the original manuscript. (All three of these methods of inserting revisions are found in extant Elizabethan manuscripts of revised plays.) She finds that many instances of textual irregularity are found in "passages which impart to the play its philosophic depth. When the origin of these misprinted passages can be traced at all, it is rarely to the primary sources." Because of systematic patterns of irregularity in the Quarto text, Doran concludes that the manuscript underlying the Quarto "appears to have been a much simpler thing when it first came into being, and to have grown in meaning as Shakespeare wrote and thought about it."[15] Doran argues that Shakespeare's work on *King Lear* grew through a process of revision, that the Quarto reproduces one stage of the composition process (and that the Folio represents the final form of the play rather than a partial transmission of a lost, perfect original). The standard and most widely accepted objection to Doran's argument is presented briefly by Greg: "The theory had to meet the difficulty of believing that Shakespeare, and that at the height of his powers, could ever have written the clumsy and fumbling lines we find in Q, or that these could in general represent a stage in the development of F" (*First Folio*, p. 379). On close examination, however, Greg's specific examples from the Quarto are not very compelling (see below, chapter 6).

Doran's theory on the derivation of the Quarto text has not received much attention from recent critics or editors. Doran herself later rejected some of her conclusions about the precise nature of the copy behind the Quarto text, saying, "My own position . . . that the quarto represents Shakespeare's much-revised autograph now appears to me dubious."[16] Nevertheless, Doran still maintains that "whether the text of Q1 as it stands is original or derivative, it still must represent an earlier form of the play than the Folio."[17]

Doran's theory, in conjunction with McKerrow's argument about foul papers used as the copy for printed play quartos, and Walker's theory of illicit copying and unauthorized printing, all justify a working presumption that the Quarto text is at least an approximation of Shakespeare's draft of the play before it was adapted for the stage.

The Second Quarto

In 1619, the First Quarto was reprinted in the same shop that was later to produce the First Folio. The copy used to compose this printing was the printed text of the First Quarto, and there are no signs that the printer referred to any other authoritative source for corrections or improvements. In the course of his work, however, the compositor made many revisions of spelling, grammar, and punctuation.[18] Some of his improvements are quite good, but they have no real authority. Through his consistent habits of spelling and typesetting, he has been identified (with reasonable certainty) as Jaggard's Compositor B, who later set a large part of *King Lear* in the Folio.[19]

The Folio

Like the critical opinions concerning the Quarto text of *King Lear*, the basic suppositions about the First Folio text have shifted considerably over the last several decades as bibliographic and literary scholars have reevaluated strongly held but fundamentally unsound textual theories. The two most important current discussions of the Folio text end by calling for more basic research into the problems of this text in the face of the present inadequacy of explanations.[20]

The monumental labors of the textual critics working on *King Lear* reveal that there are three fundamental questions which, although interrelated, must be carefully distinguished and separately addressed if any clarity is to be achieved in the overall analysis of the Folio text. Two of these questions require bibliographic interpretation of the most demanding and elegant order, and the third calls for literary and dramatic analysis applied with careful attention to the rules of bibliographic evidence and probability.

The first question concerns the actual printing of the Folio text. How did the compositors who worked on *King Lear* habitually treat their copy when they set it? Charlton Hinman's *Printing and Proof-Reading of the First Folio of Shakespeare* makes an immense contribution toward the answer to this question. (Hinman's discussion of the role of Compositor E in setting the Folio text of *King Lear* overwhelms one by the explanatory capacity of bibliographic analysis.) But Hinman recognizes that his work so far has only outlined the extent of the problems yet to be studied: "Editors of the Tragedies, and especially of *King Lear*, should take note of [Compositor] E's share in this part of the Folio; . . . they should analyse E's labours qualitatively, with particular attention to the kinds of errors to which he was most prone; and . . . they should not persist in confusing his work with [Compositor B's]" (I, 226). Far from thinking that he has reached any acceptable conclusion about the printing of the Folio text, Hinman himself sees that the task of bibliographic analysis is only now ready to begin. He says about the state of Folio-compositor study, "A systematic redrawing of the whole picture (so much of it, that is, as has already been sketched in) is therefore required" (II, 512).

The second major bibliographic question concerns the copy that was supplied to the compositors. What was it, and how reliably did it reflect the promptbook? Critics at least tentatively agree that someone acting editorially brought a version of the already printed Quarto matter into agreement with a playhouse acting version, perhaps by annotating in the margins of the Quarto, or by inserting slips of paper with required changes, or by cutting and pasting up sections of the Quarto on new sheets of paper. Several deductions about the soundness of this heterogeneous copy may safely be made. First, the editor who prepared the text to be used by the printing house was probably working from a very clear text, since the playhouse prompt copy, when in use to prompt an actor who forgot his lines, had to be readily legible. Second, the editor apparently left few indecipherable tangles, since the compositors working from this copy did not have to resort to the setting of nonsense, as their predecessors did when they set the severely confusing parts of the Quartos.[21] Third, from the number and fine details of the changes recorded by the editor it seems that he was very attentive to his task.

Much ingenuity has been demonstrated in attempts to uncover the precise details of the copy used to set the Folio text of *Lear*.[22] Nevertheless, the tentative conclusions reached by earlier critics must be examined anew in the light of Hinman's work on the compositors of the Folio text. With considerations of due caution, however, this study will proceed on the basis that the Folio is a generally accurate reproduction of a promptbook which at some time regulated performances in the Globe playhouse.

The third major question about the Folio text leads to an examination of the Quarto and the Folio as distinct dramatic documents. What are the theatrical differences between the two texts? May we observe what changes were made in the foul-paper manuscript in order to prepare it for stage presentation? All critics agree that the Folio represents a stage version of the play, though they differ about when and under whose supervision the revised text was made. In any case, the variants found in the Folio, particularly in major cuts and additions as well as the alterations in stage directions, may confidently be considered as theatrical adaptations. If this is so, then they provide valuable data for an analysis of the working methods of Shakespeare's acting company. While the promptbook that was the basis of the Folio was being prepared, what were the dramatic or literary values in the foul papers that were preserved, and what values were thought of as being less important and therefore vulnerable to change?

In the past, the Folio and Quarto texts have been used primarily in attempts to recover the *author's* original or *his* final version, supposedly approximated by the modern composite text. In their search for this ideal text, critics have not given due consideration to what may be learned about the two early texts that exist. Although the Quarto and the Folio texts of *King Lear* certainly reveal much about the lost Shakespearean drafts, they are richly endowed with untapped and even unnoticed stores of facts about revision related to producing the play. In this, as in most other ways, *King Lear* offers an extraordinary opportunity for research. The complexity, variety, and extent of textual change illustrated in two texts of reasonably good authority is, as this study will show, unparalleled.

One further question arises from any consideration of the differences between the foul papers and the promptbook. Who made the changes? Was the bookkeeper, the company working as an ensemble, or the playwright himself responsible for final polishing and pruning? E. K. Chambers presents the conventional (and certainly the most practical) response to lightly ventured speculations on this subject: "In the main we probably have to do with ordinary theatrical cutting. It is not unintelligent. . . . It is idle to ask whether Shakespeare himself or a colleague made these cuts" (*Facts and Problems*, 1, 467). Most textual critics and editors agree with Chambers's counsel of prudence. However, recent bibliographic and literary studies have forced important and extreme reversals upon some of the most basic premises of conventional textual analysis. It would be wise to examine the possibility that differences between the two early texts of *King Lear* may be the result of Shakespeare's own revision.[23] The primary task of this study is to examine the theatrical qualities of the Quarto and the Folio texts of *King Lear*.

CHAPTER II

Textual Variants in Dramatic Contexts

> Instructions to the actors are always found built into the text, rooted in the words selected, and our notion of Shakespeare as a director starts from that.
>
> J. L. Styan

> *Enter Hieronimo, he knocks up the curtaine.*
> *Enter the Duke of Castile.*
> Cast. How now, Hieronimo, where's your fellowes,
> That you take all this paine?
> *Hier.* O sir, it is for the Authors credite,
> To looke that all things may goe well:
>
> Thomas Kyd[1]

Because Shakespeare was a leading actor in a busy repertory company, he knew the strengths of his fellow actors, the range of responses of his audience, and especially the presentational resources of movement and visual display in his theater. Studies by J. L. Styan, Bernard Beckerman, and others demonstrate many of the ways Shakespeare uses dialogue to direct physical action and spatial arrangements of actors on his stage—usages making stage dialogue basically different from language found in nondramatic literature. In the two texts of *King Lear*, lines added, cut, or altered that may seem to make only slight literary difference can, however, signal radical changes in performance. Thus the significance of a variant in *Lear* should not be estimated by comparison to analogous variants in other literary forms. Instead, the variants must be evaluated within their dramatic contexts.

The purpose of this study is to demonstrate that the major variants in *King Lear* are the result of careful revision performed by a theater artist, most probably Shakespeare himself. Variants in the Folio text introduce complex changes in characterization, as well as simpler adjustments in the rhythms and the sense of dialogues. Major variants also create new designs for individual scenes and for the succession of scenes. Other significant variants present revised instructions to individual actors and to groups of actors for their entrances and exits. These variants do not resemble the kinds usually ascribed to copyists, compositors, or other agents in relatively simpler cases of textual transmission. With only one or two exceptions, these major variants may be seen as intentional revisions, in the light of the ordinary dramatic practices of Shakespeare and his acting company.

If Shakespeare was responsible for the major textual changes in *King Lear*, then the nature of his work is now inadvertently disguised in the version printed by modern editors. For example, the scene in which Gloucester brings Lear, Kent, the Fool, and Edgar to temporary shelter from the storm (3.6) consists of approximately one hundred lines in the Quarto version. The Folio text retains only half these lines of the Quarto, while combining several of the Quarto speeches into one, and adding some new speeches at the points where the major cuts of Quarto material were made. The scene in the Folio, about sixty lines long, is very quickly begun and finished. This might be seen as a reasonable theatrical revision, designed to sustain the rapid sequence of actions in this part of the play rather than allowing the pace to slow down as it does here in the Quarto version. The modern text, however, contains all the lines from the Quarto as well as those added in the Folio, producing a scene which is longer than the Quarto and more than twice as long as the Folio version. Although the modern version offers all the words that Shakespeare wrote for the scene, the reader is given little indication that the two early texts present significantly different dramatic designs. The reader certainly is not encouraged to read one version and then the other.

Dramatic texts should be carefully distinguished from other types of literary works. A poem or a novel is an artifact, a play is not. The poem must be examined as it appears on the page; only the words need be presented for us to say that the poem exists for our enjoyment and our study. In contrast, the script of a play is only the plan for a series of events. The events must be produced by actors and technicians in the presence of an audience before the play may be said to have taken place. A frequently drawn analogy compares a script to an orchestral score, since both have to be performed before the work that they represent may be experienced. Scripts seem more easy to interpret than scores, however, because they are notated in familiar literary forms—letters, words, sentences, lines of verse. No one would think that he has heard a symphony after reading through its score, but the popularity of play texts as literature leads many people to believe that they may "know" a play simply by reading its script.

Even a subject as thoroughly studied as Elizabethan rhetoric yields fresh or even alarming surprises when examined in the context of writing designed for stage presentation. When the playwright uses literary devices in his dramatic material the literary may be transfigured simply because it may be experienced in a changing context of vivid color, sound, and motion on the stage. The straightforward dramatic use of the rhetorical figure aposiopesis, a sudden breaking off of a sentence for emotional emphasis, exemplifies a device that is sometimes perfectly consonant with nondramatic usages:

> I will have such revenges on you both,
> That all the world shall———I will do such things,
> What they are yet, I know not, but they shalbe
> The terrors of the earth?[2]
>
> [Folio, 1579-82; 2.4.279-82]

In a monologue or within a long speech the interruption of a regular grammatical pattern signals that the speaker is in the throes of some passion. The device calls attention to the internal state of the speaker. However, if a speech is broken off in the course of a dialogue a different effect is achieved. The interruption then indicates a state of tension existing in a relationship. Such an interrupted speech points to a dramatic situation *between* characters. The interchange between Regan and Oswald in 4.5, as she questions him about the relationship of Goneril and Edmund, illustrates one possible use of an interrupted speech in the context of a dialogue:

> *Reg.* . . . Let me unseale the Letter.
> *Stew.* Madam, I had rather——
> *Reg.* I know your Lady do's not love her Husband,
> [Folio, 2408-10; 4.5.22-23]

Regan's speech makes the audience peculiarly aware of both the moment of transition or interruption and the words immediately following it, because the conventional and expected conclusion to Oswald's line is cut off. In this case, both the steward's reticence and Regan's urgency appear more sharply than they would if Oswald's line read, "Madam, I had rather not."

The effect of such an interruption on the audience adds an extra theatrical "dimension." At the instant when a character breaks into an ongoing speech or conversation, the audience seems to split its attention in a complex manner between two centers of interest or two characters. Instead of the regular progression of simple dialogue, in which attention shifts naturally from one speaker to the next at the ends of speeches, an interrupting speech seems to encourage the audience to watch both speakers at the same time. One might argue that an interruption of a sentence within a single speech concentrates attention on the emotions of that speaker—a single focus. In contrast, the interruption of a sentence by a succeeding speech abruptly expands the audience's attention to try to encompass nearly simultaneous events occurring along an axis joining the two speakers. At the moment of interruption in a dialogue, *both* ends of the axis are important.

I have observed in theaters that each member of the audience independently alternates his or her focus of attention from one actor to the other at the moment of an interrupted speech in a dialogue. In "linear" modes of discourse, such as the novel or the film, the narrator or the film director "calls the shots."[3] The audience sees only what the narrator speaks of or what the camera focuses upon. In contrast, one of the inherent resources of the theater is that it allows and encourages the spectators to create complex observations of their own.

The theoretical difficulty encountered in discussions such as this is that critical vocabularies are not very well suited to the analysis of events "in transit."[4] Readers tend to isolate a dramatic speech or a scene because on a printed page these stand as clearly marked and discrete entities. In contrast, members of a theater audience must experience the speeches and scenes within a continuum which allows no stopping. One might say that an irreducible element of the dramatic medium is the flow of time itself. A play is a delicate framework erected in time. The playwright controls the rhythms of events, dwelling on some, then jamming many into one breathtaking instant, then pausing upon a silence. Medieval and Renaissance playwrights were able to indicate complex intervals and transitions between stage actions within the conventions of theatrical dialogue. Although the same theatrical potentialities are being used today, some of the conventions of notation used by playwrights of the past are now unfamiliar to actors, directors, and editors.

Mistaken as accidental quirks resulting from copying or printing, several consistently notated patterns of theatrical cueing are imbedded in the dialogue of the Quarto and Folio texts of *King Lear*. Because their significance is not recognized by editors and textual critics, these important components of the playwright's art sometimes disappear when a modern text is regularized according to criteria better suited to purely literary works.

Two important items in Shakespeare's artistic vocabulary suffer significant distortion in modern texts if they occur as part of or in proximity to textual variants. First, editors frequently misunderstand purposeful interruptions, those abrupt but certainly planned disruptions of expected patterns. Sometimes these are broken patterns of words, and sometimes they are established and then broken patterns of movement seen on the stage. Second, editors fail to consider the playwright's exercise of control over his "stage pictures," the arrangement of actors on the stage as dictated by the dialogue. This control is especially fine in *King Lear* during entrances and exits within a scene, and truly extraordinary during the moments when one scene flows into the next. However, when these two kinds of information are to be found in different forms, particularly in the Quarto and the Folio of *King Lear*, they are usually treated as being of no major significance. The remainder of this chapter discusses interrupted actions as patterns in Shakespeare's plays and examines their appearance in three alternative texts of *King Lear*: the Quarto, the Folio, and the modern composite version.

Interrupted actions exist in all forms of literature as surprising patterns of narrative events, grammatical structures, or rhetorical devices. An author establishes some expectation in his audience, suddenly interrupts the flow of events, words, or images which would satisfy that expectation, and then develops unexpected consequences arising from the interruption. Interrupted speeches, the simplest of this kind of surprise, appear even in the earliest of Shakespeare's plays. Two particularly vivid examples from *3 Henry VI* indicate how one actor must break into the other actor's line:

Clifford. . . . The sight of any of the House of Yorke,
Is as a furie to torment my Soule:
And till I root out their accursed Line,
And leave not one alive, I live in Hell.
Therefore- - -
Rutland. Oh let me pray, before I take my death:
             [Folio, *3 Henry VI*, 432-37; 1.3.31-36]

Hen[ry]. . . . Teeth had'st thou in thy head, when thou was't borne,
To signifie, thou cam'st to bite the world:
And if the rest be true, which I have heard,
Thou cam'st———
Rich. Ile heare no more:
Dye Prophet in thy speech,   *Stabbes him*.
             [Folio, *3 Henry VI*, 3127-32; 5.6.53-58]

Clearly indicated by a dash or a row of three hyphens, these interrupted speeches illustrate what might be considered a dramatic "figure." The figure itself encompasses two speeches: the actor delivering the first speech must appear to be in the midst of a continuing sentence; the second actor breaks in and "takes the stage." The second speech must be strong enough to change the expected direction of the dialogue. The interrupted speech is an elementary dramatic device; actors learn it easily, and after only a little practice perform it flawlessly.

Although the appearance of an interrupted speech may be marked in a text by the same kind of dash, and though it may occur in an obviously appropriate dramatic context, some editors mistakenly see interrupted speeches as instances of textual corruption. For example, the following interrupted speech from *1 Henry VI* is much like the earlier cited instances:

> *Bed[ford].* . . . Henry the Fift, thy Ghost I invocate:
> Prosper this Realme, keepe it from Civill Broyles,
> Combat with adverse Planets in the Heavens;
> A farre more glorious Starre thy Soule will make,
> Then Julius Caesar, or bright- - - -
> *Enter a Messenger*
> *Mess.* My honourable Lords, health to you all:
> Sad tidings bring I to you out of France,
> [Folio, *1 Henry VI*, 61-68; 1.1.52-57]

When seen as a dramatic figure, the "irregular" succession of speeches highlights the disruptive nature of the messenger's news from France. Unmindful of this possibility, Andrew S. Cairncross, in the Arden edition, comments on Bedford's speech, "The F dash probably indicates the illegibility of the copy or MS," and John Dover Wilson calls this a "curious gap . . . which must have been filled up in the player's part."[5] If experienced textual critics fail to notice the dramatic function of even a simple interrupted speech in a relatively uncomplicated textual situation, then it is certainly understandable that the more subtle usages found in the complicated text of *King Lear* should have escaped any clear explication.

One group of variants in interrupted speeches in *Lear* contains particularly vivid examples of this dramatic device. The variants display complex alterations in the staging of the dialogue as well as careful adjustments in the sense of the speeches themselves. The first example discussed below illustrates the extraordinary dramatic and bibliographic complexity that may result from a seemingly simple textual change.

At a moment of shocking intensity, part of the "century" of soldiers sent by Cordelia discovers Lear on the heath in the company of Edgar and Gloucester (4.6). The Quarto presents one version of this action:

> *Lear* . . . . & when I have stole upon these sonne in lawes, then kill,kill,kill,kill,kill,kill.
> *Enter three Gentlemen.*
> *Gent.* O here he is, lay hands upon him sirs, your most deere
> *Lear.* No reskue, what a prisoner,
> [Quarto, I4^v; 4.6.186-90]

The king sees three gentlemen closing in on him, and he does not know whom they serve. They must be a frightening vision to the old king, appearing unexpectedly at the moment he is wildly visualizing the destruction of his sons-in-law. In his alarm, or as a carry-over of his homicidal excitement, Lear interrupts the Gentleman. As a bibliographic problem, one must note there is no closing punctuation of any sort at the end of the Gentleman's speech. If there were no other texts, the accidental omission of words meant to complete the speech might be suspected.

In the Second Quarto, Compositor B simply cut the uncompleted part of the speech entirely when he set it. As a result of this compositorial editing, no part of the Gentleman's abbreviated speech is addressed to Lear: "O here he is, lay hands upon him sirs."[6] However, when the same compositor, B, set the Folio version of this passage, the copy from which he worked must have contained clearer indications of what the script intended. The dramatic actions dictated and implied by what Compositor B set in the Folio text are quite different from those of both the First and the Second Quartos:

> *Lear.* . . . kill,kill,kill,kill,kill,kill.
>   *Enter a Gentleman.*
> *Gent.* Oh heere he is: lay hand upon him, Sir.
> Your most deere Daughter———
> *Lear.* No rescue? What, a Prisoner?
>   [Folio, 2629-33; 4.6.186-91]

In this version there are only four men involved—Lear, Edgar, Gloucester, and the single Gentleman—rather than the six found in the Quarto. If the Quarto text had been performed, the Gentleman's command to "lay hands upon" the king would almost certainly have been directed to his own companions, the two other gentlemen. In the performing text recorded in the Folio, however, the Gentleman must address his command to Edgar instead, since he is the only other able-bodied man onstage. The small grammatical changes in the speech are perfectly clear once this change of address is noticed. "Hands" is altered to "hand," and "sirs" becomes "Sir" in the Folio, because only one person is being addressed.

"Daughter," the additional word at the end of the Gentleman's speech, may have been in the copy for the Quarto text. We have no way of knowing. But interesting interpretations arise from the coincidence that the word was added at the same time the two supernumerary gentlemen were cut. In the Quarto text as it now stands, Lear is alarmed only by the sight of the soldiers coming to capture him. In the absence of any additional gentlemen in the Folio, however, Lear's response may be thought to be motivated primarily by the new word in the Gentleman's speech, "Daughter." Lear has no indication of which daughter this gentleman serves, but a summons from any one of them might induce him to beg for merciful treatment. The change in dramatic conception of this moment is that the physical threat generated in Lear's mind by the two other gentlemen in the Quarto is replaced in the Folio by a mental terror, the *idea* of "Daughter." Lear's response is the same, but the motivating stimulus is altered.

A further contextual difference related to the cutting of the two supernumerary gentlemen must be considered. Lear flees, but the Gentleman pauses, first to contemplate the king's fall from majesty and then to speak with Edgar:

> *Lear.* . . . I am a King, Masters, know you that?
> *Gent.* You are a Royall one, and we obey you.
> *Lear.* Then there's life in't. Come, and you get it,
> You shall get it by running: Sa, sa, sa, sa. *Exit.*
> *Gent.* A sight most pittifull in the meanest wretch,
> Past speaking of in a King. Thou hast a Daughter
> Who redeemes Nature from the generall curse
> Which twaine have brought her to.
> *'Edg.* Haile gentle Sir.
> *Gent.* Sir, speed you: what's your will?
> [Folio, 2642-51; 4.6.199-208]

In the Quarto, the two mute players may chase after Lear immediately. But in the Folio the king runs, unpursued, while the solitary Gentleman thinks and talks. This does seem strange, but the Gentleman's revery and his elaborately courteous conversation with Edgar appear to agree with the other bizarre actions, entrances, transformations, and surprises out on the heath. The Quarto certainly permits the more "practical" action, while the Folio underscores the fantastic or dreamlike pattern of events in the scene.

The above argument does not concern the overall "meaning" of *King Lear*. It is simply intended to make some sense of a variant in terms of the concerns of actors and directors. Clearly, the person who constructed the passage as it is in the First Quarto was designing the speeches and the action with the idea of having three gentlemen to work with. Whoever was responsible for the alterations in the Folio carefully redesigned the speeches and actions in order to perform the passage with only a single gentleman. Compositor B, setting the Second Quarto, acted as a nontheatrical editor and eliminated the interruption.

Modern editors emend the texts at this point by conflation and by altering the punctuation. The modern version, practically identical in all modern texts, reads:

Lear. . . . kill,kill,kill,kill,kill,kill.
        Enter a Gentleman [with Attendants].
Gent. O, here he is: Lay hand upon him.—Sir,
Your most dear daughter- - -
  Lear. No rescue? What, a prisoner?

The variants "Sir-sirs" and "hand-hands" in the early texts give interpretive cues to the actor playing the Gentleman. If the modern editors wish to follow the Quarto by providing additional "attendants," then they should also follow the Quarto usages of "hands" and "sirs." The modern text also joins "Sir" to the following sentence, making it part of an address to Lear. In recent editions the emendation is given without explanation. Perhaps one may argue that "decorum" dictates that some kind of formal salutation must precede an address to Lear. There is no basis for this change. Quite as accidentally and with the same good intentions Compositor B must have had when he set the Second Quarto, modern editors obliterate a fine dramatic point. Nothing is gained, and the dramatic integrity of both early versions is squandered.

While it may be felt that this passage shows nothing other than a playhouse alteration made for the purpose of eliminating two supernumerary characters, a similar variant where Gloucester enters to apprehend Edgar in 2.1 shows that supernumerary players might be added as well as cut in the course of refining the context of an interrupted speech. Dramatic sense rather than possible expense seems to dictate both of these changes. In the passage below, taken from the Quarto, Gloucester breaks into Edmund's third speech in order to send men in pursuit of Edgar:

        Enter Glost.
Glost. Now Edmund where is the villaine?
  Bast. Here stood he in the darke, his sharpe sword out, warbling of wicked charms, conjuring the Moone to stand's auspicious Mistris.   *Glost.* But where is he?
  Bast. Looke sir, I bleed.
  Glost. Where is the villaine Edmund?

> *Bast.* Fled this way sir, when by no means he could- - -
> *Glost.* Pursue him, go after, by no meanes, what?
> *Bast.* Perswade me to the murder of your Lordship,
> [Quarto, D3ᵛ-D4; 2.1.37-44]

There is nothing unusual in Gloucester's cry "Pursue him, go after" being directed to offstage pursuers. The Folio version of this passage makes two slight changes. First, Gloucester enters accompanied by "Servants with Torches." Just as the threatening presence of the additional gentlemen in 4.6 is transformed into an imaginary fright when they are removed, the threat of pursuit in 2.1 is made more real in the Folio by bringing the pursuers onto the stage. Further, Gloucester's interrupting speech is made more energetic by the added exclamation, "ho," in the Folio version: "Pursue him, ho: go after." These changes don't alter meanings, but they intensify the experience of the moment.

A more complex interaction between textual variants and dramatically interrupted speeches appears in 4.2, where in the various editions four distinct versions of an interrupted speech serve to cut off the bitter dialogue between Albany and Goneril. The duke and duchess have been exchanging abusive remarks about one another's general human worth. Albany, in the Quarto text, tells his wife that only her woman's shape restrains him from tearing her flesh and bones. Goneril begins a reply, interrupted as Albany notices the entrance of a gentleman:

> *Gon.* O vaine foole!
> *Alb.* Thou changed, and selfe-coverd thing for shame
> Be-monster not thy feature, wer't my fitnes
> To let these hands obay my bloud,
> They are apt enough to dislecate [*sic*] and teare
> Thy flesh and bones, how ere thou art a fiend,
> A womans shape doth shield thee.
> *Gon.* Marry your manhood now- - -
> *Alb.* What newes.   *Enter a Gentleman.*
> *Gent.* O my good Lord the Duke of Cornwals dead,
> [Quarto, H4, uncorrected state[7]; 4.2.61-70]

As in the example cited earlier from *1 Henry VI*, the entrance of this messenger should be urgent and abrupt because it appears in conjunction with an interrupted speech.

While this sheet of the First Quarto was being run off in the printing house, a press correction was made, altering Goneril's line to read, "Marry your manhood mew- - -," instead of "Marry your manhood now- - -." The punctuation of the corrected version remained unchanged, and it is still consistent with the way speech interruptions were indicated at other places in the text. As it stands in either the corrected or the uncorrected form in the Quarto, Goneril's speech is designed so that she appears ready to launch another verbal attack on her husband. She delivers only the first four words before the messenger enters and Albany interrupts her.

Modern editions present a third version of this exchange, disguising the interrupted speech figure by revising its punctuation. "Mew" is set off by almost all modern editors as if it were meant to be an interjection. The Pelican edition, for example, reads, "Marry, your manhood—mew!" and the New [Cambridge] Shakespeare offers, "Marry, your manhood! mew!" The New Arden editor gives this explanation of the speech: *"mew!*] the word is often used as an interjection; and here Goneril, by imitating a cat's noise, suggests that Albany is effeminate." "Mew" can indeed be used as an interjection. But throughout the rest of the play, Goneril typically attacks those who stand in her way; teasing is not her style. I have seen several prestigious stage productions influenced by this modern interpretation of the line, and Goneril appeared slightly ridiculous making strange catlike sounds at a moment when she should be most threatening. The modern version is a speculative rewriting of a perfectly Shakespearean moment of transition from one dramatic exchange to another.[8]

The fourth version of this passage, found in the Folio text, omits many lines but increases the excitement and alters the relationship between Goneril and Albany. Forty lines in the Quarto are reduced to only twelve in the Folio:

Enter Albany.
Gon. I have beene worth the whistle.
Alb. Oh Gonerill,

You are not worth the dust which the rude winde
Blowes in your face.
  Gon. Milke-Liver'd man,
That bear'st a cheeke for blowes, a head for wrongs,
Who hast not in thy browes an eye-discerning
Thine Honor, from thy suffering.
  Alb. See thy selfe divell:
Proper deformitie seemes not in the Fiend
So horrid as in woman.
  Gon. Oh vaine Foole.
              Enter a Messenger.
  Mes. Oh my good Lord, the Duke of Cornwals dead,
              [Folio, 2299-2313; 4.2.29-70]

Goneril's second speech, beginning "Milke-Liver'd man," is cut off by Albany. In the Quarto text, Albany rather than Goneril seems to express the greater sense of frustration, particularly when he speaks of the repressed violence he feels. Here, however, when Albany breaks into Goneril's long and insulting preamble, he effectively reduces her to uninspired, frustrated name-calling. In the Folio, Albany's stroke of rhetoric ends the feud. Only then does the messenger enter.

Of the four versions, the Folio's is the most vigorous and theatrical. It is fierce and quick. In the much longer Quarto versions, the altercation between Albany and Goneril is not resolved; it is broken off abruptly by the entrance of the messenger. The modern version disguises the urgency of the messenger's entrance found in the Quarto and the power of Albany's crushing interruption of Goneril in the Folio.

A second example of an interrupted speech that exists in only one of the texts appears in the Folio version of 3.1 during the exchange between Kent and a Gentleman in the storm. Because it occurs in an extremely complicated and textually important passage in *Lear*, it will be discussed in the fourth chapter along with other variants in the same scene.

The conventional approach to the variants thus far discussed is limited for one basic reason. Editors sometimes deal with interrupted speeches as if every speech in a play were a self-contained or discrete unit of composition. But many interrupted speeches are clearly designed as parts of dramatic figures that require the cooperation of several actors and include more than one speech. The dramatic intention behind these textual "curiosities" is lost or disguised if the single speech is not examined within its intricate context.

Although not variants themselves, two interrupted speeches in the first scene of the play illustrate the most important and consistent qualities of these theatrical figures of dialogue. The interruptions serve as signposts or motivating impulses for significant dramatic changes. The first example, quoted below, either marks or motivates Lear's turn away from Cordelia toward the rest of his court. The attention of the audience has been concentrated on the dialogue between Lear and Cordelia for a space of forty lines. Lear's address to Cordelia, "Now our Joy," begins at TLN 88 (1.1.82), and the exchange ends at TLN 128 (1.1.120), when Kent addresses Lear but is cut off. Lear then no longer speaks to Cordelia.

> *Lear.* . . . The barbarous Scythian,
> Or he that makes his generation messes
> To gorge his appetite, shall to my bosome
> Be as well neighbour'd, pittied, and releev'd,
> As thou my sometime Daughter.
>   *Kent.* Good my Liege.
>   *Lear.* Peace Kent,
> Come not betweene the Dragon and his wrath,
> I lov'd her most, and thought to set my rest
> On her kind nursery. Hence and avoid my sight:
> So be my grave my peace, as here I give
> Her Fathers heart from her; call France, who stirres?
> Call Burgundy, Cornwall, and Albanie,
> With my two Daughters Dowres, digest the third,
>   [Folio, 123-36; 1.1.116-28]

Lear will address only one more speech to Cordelia in the remainder of the scene. The figure of the interrupted speech signals the change from a tight focus upon Cordelia to a scattered and shifting attention paid to various people on the stage. (Modern editions properly indicate that Kent's speech, "Good my Liege," is incomplete, interrupted by Lear.)

In the passage quoted below, Kent again tries to address the king, and again he is interrupted. (Lear breaks into Kent's speech after ". . . in my praiers.") This interruption, unlike the first, triggers a sharp and surprising reaction from Kent. His second speech is not like the courteous preamble that Lear interrupts:

> *Kent.* Royall Lear,
> Whom I have ever honor'd as my King,
> Lov'd as my Father, as my Master follow'd,
> As my great Patron thought on in my praiers.
>   *Le.* The bow is bent & drawne, make from the shaft.
>   *Kent.* Let it fall rather, though the forke invade
> The region of my heart, be Kent unmannerly,
> When Lear is mad, what wouldest thou do old man?
> [Folio, 148-55; 1.1.139-46]

Kent's fierce reply to Lear's warning is a total change from the extremely polite manner that Kent exhibits in the opening dialogue with Gloucester and Edmund. (For a "naive" audience this comes as a shocking surprise; there is no prior expectation that Kent is a blunt or incautiously straightforward character.) These two interrupted speeches—the first marking a turn from a tightly focused exchange out to a larger discourse, and the second stimulating a turn from ornate courtesy to harsh honesty—seem to be part of the basic design of the entire scene.

The continuation of the exchange between Lear and Kent contains an important instance of an interrupted stage action, a dramatic figure related to the interrupted speech but even more difficult as a problem for textual critics and editors. The passage appears in variant forms in the Quarto and Folio:

> *Lear.* Now by Appollo,
> *Kent.* Now by Appollo King thou swearest thy Gods
> in vaine.
> *Lear.* Vassall, recreant.
> *Kent.* Doe, kill thy Physicion.
> [Quarto, B3; 1.1.160-63]

> *Lear.* Now by Apollo,
> *Kent.* Now by Apollo, King
> Thou swear'st thy Gods in vaine.

Lear. O Vassall! Miscreant.
Alb. Cor. Deare Sir forbeare.
Kent. Kill thy Physition,
   [Folio, 172-77; 1.1.160-63]

It is sometimes necessary to work backwards from the words spoken subsequent to an action in order to reconstruct the design of the action itself. To make sense out of Kent's line, "Kill thy Physition," it is reasonable to suppose that after Kent interrupts Lear's speech beginning "Now by Apollo," the king finally reacts to Kent's continued offensiveness by coming to kill him.

The Quarto and Folio agree that Lear's violent action is initiated, but they offer different plans for the completion of this stage movement. Following the Quarto text, Lear somehow advances threateningly toward Kent. The king halts because Kent brazenly stands up to him. As far as the text indicates, Lear is stopped by nothing other than Kent's forcefully stressed speech, beginning "Doe, kill thy Physicion."

Because the Folio has Albany and Cornwall interpose themselves between Lear and Kent in some way, saying "Deare Sir forbeare," Lear may attack Kent much more forcefully than in the Quarto. The actor playing Lear may rush at Kent, confident that the actors playing Albany and Cornwall have their brief line as a cue to step in and stop him.

A group of nineteenth-century promptbooks record how actors dealt with this action as it begins and is then interrupted. An anonymous Boston, Massachusetts, production, around 1830, has this instruction: "Lear, attempting to draw his sword, is prevented by Gloster [*sic*] RH and Albany LH. When Lear sheathes his sword they retire." A transcription of the promptbook for Macready's production at Covent Garden in 1838 doesn't reveal any detail about the initiation of Lear's action, but the interruption of it reads: "Albany R Cornwall L take hold of him." Similarly, Samuel Phelps' promptbook from the 1840s at Sadler's Wells instructs Albany and Cornwall to "advance R of Lear and gently stay his arm." And the most vigorous description I found, in a production by James B. Roberts in New York, 1858, reports: "Lear, seizing Axe from guard, Albany and Cornwall stop him, take Axe."[9]

The crucial point to observe is that the Quarto, the Folio, and the promptbook notations all are concerned with both the beginning *and* the ending of the action. Lear attacks Kent. And he is stopped—by Kent alone in the Quarto version, and by Albany and Cornwall according to the Folio.

"Thinking always of units of action in their sequence," J. L. Styan remarks, "Shakespeare commonly conceived an individual episode specifically to particularize a general impression through details of human behavior."[10] The actions in the Quarto vividly and graphically display Lear's sovereign willfulness and Kent's own powerful steadfastness. The sequence in the Folio shows Lear just as willful, but it adds the image of Lear being restrained by his sons-in-law (whom he had crowned and enfranchised only moments before).

An editorial tradition, begun by Rowe and continued in all modern texts, gives readers a bracketed stage direction at this point in the action. Usually, after Lear says, "O Vassall! Miscreant," editors add something like, "Lays hand on his sword," or "Starts to draw his sword." But no edition I have examined explains that this is only the beginning of a complex bit of stage business. The point of the lines is not that Lear reaches for a weapon. In fact, there is no hint in the text that the king either wears a sword or uses any kind of weapon at all. We do know, however, that Lear clearly signals his intention to kill Kent. The editorial stage direction distracts from the real action—Lear's attack and its interruption—and instead leads readers to visualize the king merely threatening or fussing with a sword and scabbard. For those unfamiliar with the athletic histrionics practiced by Shakespeare's company, this editorial suggestion fails to link the action to the responses found in the following speeches. (Better perhaps to say nothing, or to establish a separate system of reporting real theatrical stage directions from promptbooks or other records of performance.)

Since variants in *King Lear* create and alter interrupted speeches and actions, producing dramatic effects that are truly Shakespearean, these variants should not be treated either as casually or as mechanically as they have been in modern editions. Maynard Mack calls our attention to Shakespeare's "visualizing imagination, the consciousness of groupings [and] gestures."[11] Conflation, editorial revision of punctuation, and editorial stage directions inadvertently mask and distort the finely drawn patterns of dialogue and movement that are the essential life of a Shakespearean play.

In an address to the first meeting of the International Shakespeare Association in 1971, John C. Meagher cautioned: "The text to which the annotating editor of a Shakespearean play addresses himself is not a set of *disjecta membra* but a script, whose words and phrases are correlatives of moments in a dramatic context. Failure to see them in terms of this context results in the overlooking or the falsification of problems."[12] Neglect of the dramatic rather than the literary contexts of variants in the *King Lear* texts remains a serious and relatively unexamined problem in the editing of this play.

CHAPTER III

Textual Variants and Players' Entrances and Exits

> *Ja[ques]*. All the world's a stage,
> And all the men and women, meerely Players;
> They have their *Exits* and their Entrances,
>   [*As You Like It*, 1118-20; 2.7.139-41]

Entrances and exits have no counterpart in nondramatic literature, but they are among the most basic resources exploited by the playwright. In the Quarto and Folio texts of *King Lear*, textual variants associated with theatrical entrances and exits offer sharply differing plans for performance. One out of every five entrances and exits in the play appears in a significantly altered form in the two texts. In the Folio version all the entrances of actors, both individually and in groups, together number about seventy-five; exits number approximately eighty. (The discrepancy between the numbers of entrances and exits arises because characters may enter the stage separately but leave in a group, or vice versa, so a scene may not have an equal number of each.) Approximately thirty-five of the one hundred fifty-five entrances and exits differ in the two texts in ways that would be clearly noticeable in a theatrical presentation. The changes in entrances and exits involve both formal stage directions and the dialogue immediately associated with them.

Just as an interrupted speech should not be isolated from its dramatic context, a stage direction in a script may not be treated without consideration of its position within a dialogue and within the continuing progress of a play.

Entrances and exits are altered in five different ways in *King Lear*. Speeches associated with an entrance or exit may be transferred from one character to another; components of the theatrical spectacle such as music or stage properties may be added or eliminated; additions of large or small amounts of dialogue may appear; cuts within speeches, or of entire speeches, or of groups of speeches may be made; and the moment in which an entrance or exit occurs within a dialogue may be changed.

Variants in speech headings associated with entrances and exits illustrate how a strong theatrical moment in the Quarto text is altered so that the Folio version presents something quite different, but of equal dramatic validity. For example, in the Quarto text the moment of Goneril's entry into the meeting between Lear, Cornwall, and Regan in 2.4 is by any measure a vigorous piece of stagecraft. First, Lear attacks Goneril's agent, Oswald, and then Goneril enters. As soon as she appears she captures the attention of the other actors and the audience. With her bold question she "takes the stage":

> *Lear.* This is a slave, whose easie borrowed pride
> Dwels in the fickle grace of her, a followes,
> Out varlet, from my sight.
>   *Duke.* What meanes your Grace?   *Enter Gon.*
>   *Gon.* Who struck my servant, Regan I have good hope
> Thou didst not know ant.
>   *Lear.* Who comes here? O heavens!
> If you doe love old men,
>
>   [Quarto, F1ᵛ; 2.4.185-90]

Here Goneril storms into action, angry and threatening. This closely resembles her first speech in 1.3 where she also entered angrily, concerned with a nearly identical issue: "Did my Father strike my Gentleman for chiding of his Foole?" (Folio, 507-8; 1.3.1-2).

The Folio variant, however, gives Goneril's speech to Lear, joining it to his speech following. "Struck" is changed to "stockt," so the reference to "my servant" remains appropriate to the speaker. Goneril was referring to Oswald, while Lear speaks of Kent:

>   . . . Out Varlet, from my sight.
>   *Corn.* What meanes your Grace?

> *Enter Gonerill.*
> Lear. Who stockt my Servant? Regan, I have good hope
> Thou did'st not know on't.
> Who comes here? O Heavens!
> If you do love old men;
>
> [Folio, 1475-80; 2.4.187-90]

A specific dramatic effect, equally striking but differing markedly from the Quarto is achieved by the Folio. In the Quarto, the audience would have shifted its attention entirely to Goneril. But the Folio version concentrates the audience's attention instead on Lear's discovery of her entrance. The audience observes Lear's turns—from the moment he chases Oswald, to his next moment addressing Cornwall and Regan, to his next when he sees Goneril, and then finally as he turns to address the heavens. Throughout Goneril's entrance, the Folio text keeps Lear as the center of the action.

An important aspect of the dramatic effect in the Folio version is that Lear does not see Goneril until after she is seen by the audience, and probably also after the other characters on stage have noticed her arrival. (Cornwall and Regan, at least, indicate their anticipation of her entrance by their responses to the trumpet "tucket" and to Oswald's appearance.) Lear's perception is a step behind the others in the Folio.

Most modern editions, seemingly in an effort to rationalize the positioning of stage directions, move Goneril's entrance from the position it occupies in both the Quarto and the Folio to a point approximately two lines later. The Pelican edition, for example, reads:

> ... Regan, I have good hope
> Thou didst not know on't.
>   *Enter Goneril*   Who comes here? O heavens!
>
> [p. 86]

The New Arden text offers a slightly different form:

> ... Who comes here?
>   *Enter Goneril.*
>   O Heavens,
>
> [p. 95]

In either of these versions, Lear sees Goneril at the same moment as everyone else, while he is saying the longer, Folio version of his speech. This is certainly a justifiable dramatic possibility, but it is simply not one of those offered by the two authoritative texts. And it is inferior to both early versions. The modern version not only lacks the forceful and commanding entry of Goneril found in the Quarto, but it also misses the distracted and arhythmic spinning about of Lear found in the Folio. The dramatic qualities of both early versions are lost and for all practical purposes irrecoverable in these modern texts.

Other places where variants in speech headings occur in the context of entrances and exits may be found at the reentry of Gloucester at the end of 2.4 (F3 in the Quarto; TLN 1594-97 in the Folio; 2.4.293-95), at the exit of Cornwall and Regan as they leave Kent and Gloucester at the end of 2.2 (E2^v; TLN 1225-27; 2.2.150-51), and at Goneril's exit from 5.3 (L2; TLN 3112-20; 5.3.155-61). In each case, either alternative variant would have been unquestionably accepted as Shakespearean, purposeful, and theatrically intelligible if we had only one. But when one must be considered "authentic" and the other "corrupt," or when both must be juggled to recreate the "lost original," the virtues of the early texts are obscured.

Another variant speech heading associated with an entrance or exit is used in the following paragraphs to illustrate how spectacle and dialogue may be made to interact in surprising and subtle ways. Gloucester announces the entrance of France and Burgundy in the Quarto version of the play's opening scene, immediately after Kent's exit:

Thus Kent O Princes, bids you all adew,
Heele shape his old course in a countrie new.
  Enter France and Burgundie with Gloster.
Glost. Heers France and Burgundie my noble Lord.
                    [Quarto, B3^v; 1.1.186-89]

Kent's departure and the arrival of the suitors seems to take place in an undefined blending of movement in the Quarto text. Gloucester's announcement seems to mark the end of that period of transition between the two successive passages. No such vagueness appears in the Folio version:

> Thus Kent, O Princes, bids you all adew,
> Hee'l shape his old course, in a Country new.   *Exit.*
> *Flourish. Enter Gloster with France, and Burgundy, Attendants.*
> *Cor.* Heere's France and Burgundy, my Noble Lord.
> [Folio, 200-204; 1.1.186-89]

The order of events is clearly indicated by the added stage directions, *"Exit"* and *"Flourish."*

The change in the speech heading, *"Glou."* to *"Cor."* is taken by all modern editors since Theobald to be an error in the Folio. The Pelican editor, for example, expands *"Cor."* to *"Cordelia,"* and lists this speech heading among the rejected Folio readings (p. 169).

Although it may seem difficult at first glance to justify the speech in the mouth of Cordelia, *"Cor."* may very well stand for *"Cornwall."*[1] If Cornwall is considered as the speaker, then the variant speech heading leads to several plausible changes in interpretation of the plan for this action as it is offered in the Folio. Since in the Quarto Gloucester's speech is the only formal announcement of the entrance of France and Burgundy, it must focus the audience's attention on the new business. Before Gloucester "takes the stage" with his speech, the audience may, for example, look at each of the major figures to read their reactions to Kent's exit, or the audience may watch those on stage make room for the new characters. In the Folio, however, the trumpet call seems sufficient to bring all eyes to watch the entrance of the suitors. What then is the purpose of the speech, now given to Cornwall, if attention has already been brought to the arrival of France and Burgundy? The following is offered as a purely speculative interpretation based on theatrical intuition rather than hard evidence: if everyone *except* the king turns at the trumpet cue to watch the grand entrance of the suitors, and if they take their proper places in relation to Lear while he continues to stare in whatever direction he was looking during Kent's exit, and if all movement comes to a halt while the court waits for

Lear to notice that France and Burgundy are waiting, then Cornwall's speech could be a careful prodding of the dangerous king. Indeed, if such a delay is incorporated in a theatrical realization of the script, the line may even be given to Cordelia, since it is in her interest that Lear should deal with France and Burgundy. This admittedly speculative interpretation requires only that Lear should not react at the same time as everyone else, a flaw in his mental synchronization also found in the Folio version of Lear's responses to Goneril's arrival at Gloucester's castle in 2.4, discussed above. The Folio version requires some kind of dramatic daring if it is to be performed as written, but it asks for no impossibilities or violations of logic.

The modern version includes the additional flourish from the Folio text, but it follows the Quarto in its ascription of the next speech to Gloucester rather than *Cor*. The modern version is theatrically workable, but different from the early texts. Gloucester was not onstage during any of the preceding action between Lear, his daughters, and Kent. If the entrance is played as a straightforward action with no delay, as the Quarto and the modern text imply, Gloucester's line, "Here's France and Burgundy," is simply an extension of the ceremonial introduction begun by the flourish. In contrast, the Folio version, whether *Cor*. is Cornwall or Cordelia, enforces a complex "subtext" on the interpretation of the line, since the characters who were onstage to watch the division of the kingdom may no longer view the arrival of the suitors as a simple ceremony. The Folio version is not simple, but it works, and it should not be dismissed by modern editors.

The second grouping of variants associated with entrances and exits includes many additional examples of changes made only in stage spectacle. The sounds of thunder, trumpets, and drums, the visible displays of torches, weapons, and banners, and the mute figures of servants, soldiers, and gentlemen are added or, occasionally, cut in the Folio text. Martial entrances in the different versions, for example, illustrate how spectacular displays are changed for dramatic effect. The first "army" to appear in *King Lear* is Cordelia's, seen at the opening of 4.4. The Quarto's stage direction is simply:

"*Enter Cordelia, Doctor and others.*" The Folio presents a vivid display of banners, drums, and arms: "*Enter with Drum and Colours, Cordelia, Gentlemen, and Souldiours.*" Similar changes appear at the entrance of Edmund, Regan, and their army at the beginning of 5.1, and at the entrance of Albany, Goneril, and their forces later in the same scene. The detail of drum and colors appears again as an addition in the Folio version when Lear and Cordelia enter and pass over the stage without speaking in 5.2, and once again when they enter as Edmund's prisoners at the beginning of the last scene, 5.3. Although these may seem to be purely mechanical or technical adjustments, a contrasting effect is used only in the final martial entrance of the play. This triumphant entrance of Albany, Goneril, and Regan in 5.3 is heralded by a trumpet flourish in the Folio text, instead of by drums and banners. The brazen celebration of the victors sounds only a few moments after the audience observes Lear and Cordelia led off to prison and immediately after the exit of the captain sent to murder them. Trumpets with such ironic overtones are heard in the final scenes of other Shakespearean tragedies; their addition here in the Folio of *King Lear* seems to enhance the tension of this exciting moment.[2]

The Folio text also calls for the addition of hunting horns before Lear's entrance to Goneril's hall in 1.4, and a torch is provided in the Folio for Gloucester when he first finds Lear in the storm in 3.4. Conversely, the lights that both men carry in the Quarto version while Gloucester confides his secret news to Edmund in 3.3 are struck from the acting script, as is the music meant to accompany the entrance of Lear as he is carried in, asleep, to meet Cordelia in 4.7. The Folio version of this latter scene seems to strive for a simpler presentation than the Quarto version. Two speaking parts, the Doctor and a Gentleman, are combined into one. And the entrance of the king, carried in a chair, is indicated more precisely and is accomplished without musical accompaniment. The changes seem to suppress the importance of the Doctor-Gentleman as master of healing, leaving instead only Cordelia and Lear as the centers of attention.[3]

The modern text here combines material from the Quarto

and the Folio, producing a version of this passage that is perhaps slightly more complex than the Quarto. Two separate actions seem to be dictated by the modern version; first Lear is brought in and then several lines later either he is brought forward toward Cordelia or she, Kent, and the Doctor approach Lear. The theatrical consequences of the three different versions should be distinguished for readers and performers. Again, the simplest version, found in the Folio, cannot be easily extricated from the text presented by modern editions.

Insertions of short or long passages in the Folio text form the third grouping of variants related to entrances and exits in *King Lear*. Two illustrative examples may be found in Edmund's first dialogue with Edgar in 1.2. The first addition seems to be a neat theatrical embellishment: as Edgar enters, the Folio text has Edmund singing "Fa, Sol, La, Me," a progression of tones known as the *diabolus* in medieval musical theory, and appropriate to deviltry. A few lines later, the Folio text contains a more elaborate bit of energetic business worked into the dialogue where Edmund propels Edgar from the stage. The Quarto version of Edmund's speech gives him a single command, "Pray you away," with which to motivate Edgar's departure:

Edg. Some villaine hath done me wrong.
Bast. Thats my feare brother, I advise you to the best, goe arm'd, I am no honest man if there bee any good meaning towards you, I have told you what I have seene & heard, but faintly, nothing like the image and horror of it, pray you away!
Edg. Shall I heare from you anon?
Bast. I doe serve you in this busines: *Exit Edgar*
[Quarto, C2ᵛ-C3; 1.2.165-78]

In contrast, Edmund urges his brother to go off three times in the Folio text. The variants, in boldface in the passage below, allow Edmund first to begin walking out with Edgar: "retire with me to my lodging." Then Edmund stops, and sends his brother off alone with a key: "pray ye go, there's my key." But then Edmund delays Edgar's exit again when he offers further advice: "if you do stirre abroad," etc., and finally he dismisses Edgar for the last time, "pray you away," seven lines after the initial impulse for the exit was spoken.

> *Edg.* Some Villaine hath done me wrong.
> *Edm.* That's my feare, **I pray you have a continent forbearance till the speed of his rage goes slower: and as I say, retire with me to my lodging, from whence I will fitly bring you to heare my Lord speake: pray ye goe, there's my key: if you do stirre abroad,** goe arm'd.
> *Edg.* Arm'd, Brother?
> *Edm.* **Brother,** I advise you to the best, I am no honest man, if ther be any good meaning toward you: I have told you what I have seene, and heard: But faintly. Nothing like the image, and horror of it, pray you away.
> *Edg.* Shall I heare from you anon?   *Exit.*
> [Folio, 486-97; 1.2.165-77; boldface indicates matter only in Folio]

Another variant involving additional material in the Folio occurs as Albany enters to the first confrontation between Goneril and Lear in 1.4. The change seems at first minor, perhaps more in the nature of a textual correction than a theatrical elaboration:

> *Enter Duke.*
> *Lear.* We that too late repent's, O sir, are you come? is it your will that wee prepare any horses, ingratitude! thou marble harted fiend, more hideous when thou shewest thee in a child, then the Sea-monster, detested kite, thou list . . .
> [Quarto, D2; 1.4.257-62]

> *Enter Albany.*
> *Lear.* Woe, that too late repents:
> Is it your will, speake Sir? Prepare my Horses.
> Ingratitude! thou Marble-hearted Fiend,
> More hideous when thou shew'st thee in a Child,
> Then the Sea-monster.
> *Alb.* Pray Sir be patient.
> *Lear.* Detested Kite, thou lyest.
> [Folio, 768-75; 1.4.257-62]

The addition of the speech for Albany helps the actor playing the role insofar as it gives him an action to play (trying to calm the king) while he watches Lear storming about the stage. The added speech, since it interrupts Lear's address to Ingratitude, also gives the actor playing Lear a point of "dramatic punctuation" to help him turn from his apostrophe toward the spirit of ingratitude and then return to address his daughter about another issue. Thus, the relatively simple polishing of the text also aids the dramatic presentation. Further examples of this kind of variant appear in the Folio text at TLN 1807-8 (3.4.26-27), where two additional lines elaborate Lear's urging of the Fool to go into the hovel before him; at TLN 1819 (3.4.37), where a new speech for Edgar makes his the first voice to announce the eruption of Mad Tom in the play; and at TLN 2936 (5.3.11), where a speech of extraordinary simplicity and depth is supplied for Gloucester, his final utterance in the play:

> *Glo.* No further Sir, a man may rot even heere.
> *Edg.* What in ill thoughts againe?
> Men must endure
> Their going hence, even as their comming hither,
> Ripenesse is all come on.
> **Glo. And that's true too.**   *Exeunt.*
>   [Folio, 2931-36; 5.2.8-11;
>   boldface indicates matter only in Folio]

In the Quarto it appears that Gloucester accepts Edgar's philosophy in place of his own, but in the Folio Gloucester gives "ripenesse is all" only a validity equal to "a man may rot even heere."

Two very long passages associated with entrances and exits are found only in the Folio version. The simpler of the two is the Fool's prophecy at the end of Lear's first scene on the heath, 3.2. Although its authenticity has been frequently questioned in the past, it has recently been recognized as a typically Shakespearean adaptation of folk-poetry patterns and folk-drama themes developed throughout *King Lear*.[4] The second long passage only in the Folio is found in 1.4, after the Fool's exit but immediately preceding the entrance of Oswald. Fifteen continuous lines in the Folio are not in the Quarto, and several isolated phrases are altered or added. Goneril is the center of the action in both texts. The Quarto shows her in vigorous and continuous action; the Folio, by introducing a delay between the time she calls for Oswald and the time he appears, shows her thinking aloud during the intervals between her brusque commands.

> *Gon.* Doe you marke that my Lord?
> *Duke.* I cannot bee so partiall Gonerill to the great love I beare you,
> *Gon.* Come sir no more, you, more knave then foole, after your master?
> *Foole.* Nunckle Lear, Nunckle Lear, . . .
> *Gon.* What Oswald, ho.   *Oswald.* Here Madam,
> *Gon.* What have you writ this letter to my sister?
>
> [Quarto, D2ᵛ; 1.4.310-35]

> *Gon.* Do you marke that?
> *Alb.* I cannot be so partiall Gonerill,
> To the great love I beare you.
> *Gon.* **Pray you content. What Oswald, hoa?**
> You **Sir**, more Knave then Foole, after your Master.
> *Foole.* Nunkle Lear, Nunkle Lear,
> . . . .   *Exit*
>
> *Gon.* **This man hath had good Counsell,**
> **A hundred Knights?**
> **'Tis politike, and safe to let him keepe**
> **At point a hundred Knights: yes, that on everie dreame,**
> **Each buz, each fancie, each complaint, dislike,**
> **He may enguard his dotage with their powres,**
> **And hold our lives in mercy. Oswald, I say.**
> *Alb.* **Well, you may feare too farre.**
> *Gon.* **Safer then trust too farre;**
> **Let me still take away the harmes I feare,**
> **Not feare still to be taken. I know his heart,**
> **What he hath utter'd I have writ my Sister:**
> **If she sustaine him, and his hundred Knights**
> **When I have shew'd th'unfitnesse.**
>   ***Enter Steward.***

How now Oswald?
What have you writ **that** Letter to my Sister?
[Folio, 830-59; 1.4.310-35; boldface indicates matter added or changed in Folio]

Goneril abruptly questions Albany, in both texts, and in both she curtly interrupts his reply. She turns to dismiss the Fool, and she calls for Oswald. In the Quarto text he enters at once. Only after her steward is instructed and dispatched does Goneril again turn to address and admonish her husband: "get you gon & hasten your returne[;] now my Lord, this milkie gentlenes and course of yours . . ."

The Folio version delays Oswald's entrance to develop the theme of a sovereign's security being opposed to a sovereign's obligations, Goneril's safety versus Lear's hundred knights. The theatrical elaboration of the passage includes an additional speech interruption: Goneril once again interrupts her discourse with Albany. At the moment Oswald enters, she turns from Albany, never completing the sentence beginning "If she sustaine him, . . ." So even though Goneril says more to Albany in the Folio version than in the Quarto, the interrupted speech figure found in the Folio version of Oswald's entrance adds another particular instance of how Goneril dismisses her husband. For her, though he may be present, he is unimportant.

The complexity of the Folio variant in this case illustrates how actors' entrances might be made more complex as *King Lear* was revised for the stage. Simplification through theatrical cutting, however, is far more frequently found in variants associated with entrances and exits. Produced by cuts ranging from single words to an entire scene, subtle or startling effects are found in the Folio version that are not in the Quarto. Most of these dramatic effects generated by cutting are also absent from most modern texts and from modern productions based upon modern texts.

The elimination in the Folio of short speeches immediately before or after entrances and exits concentrates the attention of the audience in a new way in several important scenes. For example, a speech by Goneril at her entrance with Albany and his army in 5.1 (Quarto, K3; 5.1.18-19) is cut, leaving Albany as the sole center of interest at the moment he decides whether to enter the battle against Lear and Cordelia. (The larger context of this variant will be analyzed in Chapter 5.) A similar cut occurs immediately before Albany's entrance to 5.3 (Quarto, K4ᵛ; 5.3.38-39), where the second speech for Edmund's Captain, "I cannot draw a cart, nor eate dride oats . . ." is left out of the Folio. Instead of seeing this Captain explain his moral subjugation to the force of corrupt power, the audience watches Edmund drive him to his task, and then immediately turns to see Albany, Goneril, and Regan enter. In the Folio the Bastard is the only active figure and the important focus of attention. His agent is practically mute—a figure, not a character. Although the Quarto text gives us a Captain vividly realized in only a dozen or so words, the line seems to have been cut in order to allow Edmund to be shown, at his most villainous moment, against a neutral rather than against a lively background. Both of these cuts of single speeches at important entrances and exits demonstrate an awareness of how to control or alter the audience's perception of the "stage-picture." Both cuts remove an interesting but subsidiary detail in order to allow the main event to stand out more sharply.

This same control over the audience's focus of attention is found in six major variants created by the omission from the Folio of long passages in the Quarto associated with entrances and exits. The absence of these lines from the Folio is ascribed by all textual critics to theatrical cutting. The possible theatrical benefits of this cutting have only rarely been noticed, but the apparent literary and dramatic losses that the Folio version of the play suffers owing to the omission of this material have been stated repeatedly by editors. The modern diagnosis of the "damage" incurred by the Folio cuts has changed little from early statements of it in the eighteenth century. Kenneth Muir offers a representative analysis:

> If in producing the play you begin cutting out scenes or lines you soon come to realize how impossible it is to find

a superfluous line. Shakespeare's fellows, one hopes after his retirement, made a number of cuts. Each one is disastrous from a dramatic point of view. They cut out, for example, the mock trial of Goneril and Regan in the third act of the play, a trial which is manifestly necessary for our understanding of Lear's development, as it is essential to the symbolic pattern of the play. Then they cut out the dialogue between the two servants after the blinding of Gloucester. How much the scene would lose by the omission of this choric comment by ordinary humanity on the cruelty of Regan and Cornwall, how necessary it is to end the scene and the act quietly rather than violently, and how desirable it is to prepare the way for Poor Tom's meeting with Gloucester! Then the actors apparently omitted the whole of 4.3. . . . At first sight it seems to be a passage which could be omitted without loss. But Cordelia's part is so very short that her next appearance requires a preparation and build-up. The ineffectiveness of the Cordelia in many modern productions is largely due to the omission of this preparatory scene. Apart from that, the audience needs to be informed of the reason why Lear refuses to see Cordelia.[5]

However, a very different view is held by Harley Granville-Barker, one of the few commentators on this issue with recognized expertise and experience in actually producing this play. Granville-Barker finds sufficient theatrical reasons to advise that 4.3 and several other passages from the Quarto (though by no means all of them) be omitted from stage productions.[6] The following analysis is concerned with the consequences, not of modern theatrical cutting, but of the cuts in the Folio version of *King Lear* that would be noticed by an audience.

The first of the major cuts involving entrances and exits sharply compresses the action at the end of 3.6, where in both texts Gloucester enters, only a moment after Lear is lulled to sleep, and urges that Lear be carried away to safety at Dover. In the Quarto text the pace of the dialogue is balanced between Gloucester's nervousness on the one hand and by

Kent's gentle address to his sleeping master and Edgar's meditative cadences and rhymes on the other hand:

> *Glost.* Good friend-I prithy take him in thy armes,
> . . . .
> . . . take up thy master,
> . . . .
> Take up the King and followe me, that will to some provision
> Give thee quicke conduct.
> *Kent.* Oppressed nature sleepes,
> This rest might yet have balmed thy broken sinewes,
> Which if convenience will not alow stand in hard cure,
> Come helpe to beare thy maister, thou must not stay behind.
> *Glost.* Come, come away. *Exit.*
> *Edg.* When we our betters see bearing our woes: we scarcely thinke, our miseries, our foes.
>
> [Quarto, G4^v; 3.6.88-103]

Kent's and Edgar's speeches in the Quarto are noticeable pauses in the rushing action of this part of the play. These two speeches seem to return the audience's attention to Lear while he sleeps onstage, and again after he is carried out.

The Folio version of this passage eliminates the speeches for Kent and Edgar, and it achieves several remarkably theatrical and different results. Lear's suffering, Kent's sympathy for his master, and Edgar's isolation are the concerns of the Quarto here. In contrast, Gloucester's insistent support for Lear, in the face of danger, and then the immediate consequence of Gloucester's defiance of Cornwall in the following scene become the focus of the Folio. Without the slower rhythms of Kent's and Edgar's speeches, in the Folio the end of 3.6 and the beginning of 3.7 are both unrelievedly urgent, compelling, and threatening:

> *Glou.* Good friend, I prythee take him in thy armes;
> . . . .
> . . . Take up thy Master,
> . . . .
> . . . Take up, take up,

And follow me, that will to some provision
Give thee quicke conduct. Come, come, away.   *Exeunt*

Scena Septima.

Enter Cornwall, Regan, Gonerill, Bastard,
and Servants.
  Corn. Poste speedily to my Lord your husband, shew
him this Letter, the Army of France is landed: seeke out
the Traitor Glouster.
                         [Folio, 2047-62; 3.6.88-3.7.3]

The scene following 3.6, as may be observed in Cornwall's opening speech from 3.7 quoted above, continues unabated the rhythmic and narrative excitement of the Folio version of 3.6. The Quarto text preserves a fuller literary record of obviously Shakespearean writing, but the Folio offers a more vigorous rhythm of speeches and incidents. The modern version of this passage is compounded from both the Quarto and the Folio, but in the process of conflation the singular virtues of the Folio—its urgency and its rhythmic continuity with the following scene—are lost.

The Folio version of the final exit from 3.7 once again brings the action at the end of a scene to an impulsive rather than to a reflective transition into the next scene following.

  Reg. Go thrust him out at gates, and let him smell
His way to Dover.   *Exit with Glouster.*
How is't my Lord? How looke you?
  Corn. I have receiv'd a hurt: Follow me Lady;
Turne out that eyelesse Villaine: throw this Slave
Upon the Dunghill: Regan, I bleed apace,
Untimely comes this hurt. Give me your arme. *Exeunt,*
                         [Folio, 2170-76; 3.7.93-98]

One servant goes out leading the mutilated Gloucester, one or two others drag or carry out the corpse of the servant who tried to save Gloucester, and Cornwall, bleeding and unable to move without assistance, staggers offstage on the arm of his wife.

A dramatic coda, including an exchange of moral sentiments and a plan to aid Gloucester, appears in the Quarto version of this scene:

> *Servant.* Ile never care what wickednes I doe,
> If this man come to good.
>   *2 Servant.* If she live long, & in the end meet the old course of death, women will all turne monsters.
>   *1 Ser.* Lets follow the old Earle, and get the bedlom
> To lead him where he would, his madnes
> Allows it selfe to any thing.
>   *2 Ser.* Goe thou, ile fetch some flaxe and whites of egges to apply to his bleeding face, now heaven helpe him.   *Exit.*
> [Quarto, H2; 3.7.99-107]

The First Servant's plan is at odds with how the meeting between Gloucester and Edgar occurs in the next scene. Much more important than this technical difference between the plot as predicted in 3.7 and as it occurs in 4.1, the First Servant's statement of the plan removes the theatrical element of surprise that is clearly intended in the design of 4.1. Many indications are given that the meeting in 4.1 should be a surprise to the Old Man who is leading Gloucester, to Gloucester himself, to Edgar, and especially to the audience.

The important events in 4.1 are Gloucester's *accidental* meeting with Edgar, Gloucester's development of a plan to use the "madman" as a guide toward Dover, and Gloucester's recruitment of his son over the strenuous objections of the Old Man. The poignancy of the scene is in a large part due to its unexpected unfolding of these events. If the coda of 3.7 is omitted, as in the Folio, the audience watches Gloucester's morose entrance with the same sense of surprise and anguish reported by Edgar, "But who comes here?" The audience should perhaps feel a sense of rising hopes or expectations when Gloucester enlists Edgar's aid to go with him toward Dover, identified repeatedly in the previous scenes as the rallying point for Lear's friends. But such promising signals are then shown to be false, or at best premature, when the audience learns in Gloucester's last speech in the scene that he is not seeking friends at Dover but instead the cliffs, clearly as a place for suicide. Also, Edgar maintains his disguise as Poor Tom. He does not disclose his identity to his father, so the potential for a partially satisfying result which was suddenly generated earlier in the scene when Gloucester and Edgar were brought together is not realized by the end of the scene.[7] Much of the surprise inherent in this plan for 4.1 is prematurely revealed by the First Servant's speech found only in the Quarto text of the scene before.

Whatever value there may be in the sentiments spoken by the two servants at the end of 3.7 must be weighed against the loss of dramatic surprise in 4.1 if the cut passage is restored to the text. There is certainly more "meaning" provided by the Quarto's lines, but in a crucial sense for the audience there is less "experience," not as much "magic," fewer sensations of "drama." Removed from the context of the play, one version of 3.7 may have little to recommend it over the other, except for considerations of personal taste. But within the context of scenes that depend on one another for continuity, change, or surprise, the Folio version of 3.7 is to be preferred because it allows qualities of 4.1 to appear which are scarcely noticed in the Quarto. The Quarto text indeed provides a choric commentary, a quiet ending, and preparation for the scene to come, but these qualities are not demonstrably or theoretically superior to a tableau of servants silently obedient as they remove a corpse, a final outcry from Cornwall in pain, and a following scene filled with unexpected incident.

The next major variant produced by theatrical cutting reduces from forty lines to twelve the bitter dialogue between Albany and Goneril spoken in 4.2. The Folio preserves the basic form of the confrontation after the entrance of Albany and before the entrance of the Messenger bearing news of Cornwall's death and Gloucester's blinding. The Quarto and the Folio here again both offer "good" texts. Either might be performed without any sense that a dramatic or textual "mistake" had been made. Again, the Quarto has more lines, and the Folio gives a quicker and in some ways harsher series of actions and images. Albany loses his "sentiments" in the Folio, but the exchange crackles more energetically. The modern text, which in all editions follows the Quarto, reproduces the longer of the two alternative designs for characterization and pace in this scene.

Immediately following 4.2, the Quarto contains a scene of about sixty lines, designated 4.3 in modern editions. The entire scene is cut in the Folio; "Scena Tertia" of the fourth act in the Folio is the scene that brings Cordelia back onto the stage.[8] The Quarto scene has been included in all modern editions since Pope argued that it was "manifestly of Shakespear's writing, and necessary to continue the story of Cordelia, whose behavior here is most beautifully painted."[9] Despite its poetic beauty, and notwithstanding the long tradition of including the scene in printed editions, the interpolation of 4.3 into the text of a performing script of *King Lear* creates serious dramatic problems not found in the Folio.

One major anomaly introduced by 4.3 is Kent's description of Lear's "soveraigne shame," which, he says, keeps the king from meeting with Cordelia. But when Lear next appears onstage in 4.6 he is notably silent about Cordelia's presence in England. Though he has ample opportunity in this scene to express the "shame" ascribed to him, he does not. Further, Lear's ingenuous surprise when he awakens to discover Cordelia before him in 4.7 argues against his having any prior knowledge of her arrival from France. And the clear, humble humanity Lear expresses sounds in no way like "shame." The "news" supplied in 4.3 interferes with any direct or simple understanding of Lear's emotions at the moment of reunion.

Also, the report in 4.3 of where Lear may be found contradicts lines at the beginning of 4.4. At 4.3.38, Kent says, "Well sir, the poore distressed Lear's ith towne," and at 4.3.50-51 Kent says, "Well sir, ile bring you to our maister Lear, / And leave you to attend him" (Quarto, I). Only nine lines later, at TLN 2356-58 (4.4.6-8), Cordelia commands: "A Centery send forth; / Search every Acre in the high-growne field, / And bring him to our eye." To account for this sudden portation of the king from town to field, one modern editor notes, "Between this scene [4.4] and Scene iii Lear has wandered away, and he has to be rediscovered."[10] A surprising amount of extratextual rationalizing is required as soon as 4.3

is included as a regular part of the *Lear* text. The dramatic material found in 4.3 has many of the qualities found in the coda to 3.7; it is of poetic interest, but in the plot it is at best forgettable and at worst seriously misleading. When the scene is cut the play improves.

Another theatrical cut at the end of the scene in which Lear is brought to meet with Cordelia, 4.7, similarly removes a passage of dialogue (again between Kent and a Gentleman) that has no relationship to any action or event in the play. Also, as the result of the cutting, a pair of closely related stage-pictures in different scenes are brought closer together. Without the Quarto's exchange of speeches between Kent and a Gentleman, 4.7 ends with a procession led by Lear and Cordelia together, followed by Kent, the Gentleman who acted as doctor, and several servants bearing the chair used earlier to carry in the king. This gentle pageant of physical and familial restoration is followed abruptly in the Folio by a martial display and dialogue that returns the play to its most divisive themes—the harsh conjunction of authority and violence:

>   *Cor.* Wilt please your Highnesse walke?
>   *Lear.* You must beare with me:
>   Pray you now forget, and forgive;
>   I am old and foolish.   *Exeunt*

Actus Quintus. Scena Prima.

>   *Enter with Drumme and Colours, Edmund, Regan,*
>   *Gentlemen, and Souldiers.*
>   *Bast.* Know of the Duke if his last purpose hold,
>   [Folio, 2840-47; 4.7.81-5.1.1]

Only in the Folio version does the audience see these contrasting images immediately following one another.

Hereward T. Price identifies this kind of abrupt juxtaposition as one of the basic patterns of the playwright's work: "The effectiveness of the single scene Shakespeare further enhances by the opposition or contrast of scene with scene.

Just as he flings speech at speech, so he flings scene at scene."[11] The variants in the Folio text create new designs for the events shown to the audience at the junctures of 3.6-3.7, 3.7-4.1, 4.2-(4.3)-4.4, and 4.7-5.1. In each of these instances the changes found in the Folio increase the dramatic pace and the emotional intensity of the transition. In each case the plan adopted in the promptbook for all practical purposes passes unnoticed by readers of modern editions.

All of the cuts and some of the additions in the Folio text analyzed in this chapter are accepted by textual authorities as "theatrical." The work of adaptation, all agree, was done to prepare it for the stage. This chapter has shown that the work was done carefully, and it was done to bring the text into accord with important theatrical values—concision, contrast, and surprise.

CHAPTER IV

Interrupted Exits and the Textual Variants in Act Three, Scene One

> ... But march away,
> Hector is dead: there is no more to say.
> Stay yet:
> [*Troilus and Cressida*, Folio 3557-59; 5.10.21-23]

The two preceding chapters give some indication of how the dramatic experience depends upon stage movement dictated by cues in the dialogue and stage directions. The present chapter is addressed to the problems of textual and critical interpretation of *King Lear* arising from one kind of stage movement, the interrupted exit. Important variants in the play are found that have to do with interrupted exits. But before these textually complex examples are considered, it is necessary first to ascertain the patterns of movement, of dialogue, and of plotting associated with this theatrical device. Only then can one understand the theatrical purposes for these variants in *Lear*, which have puzzled actors, editors, and textual critics for nearly three centuries.

The interrupted exit, like the interrupted speech, is one of the basic devices for creating surprise in dramatic dialogue. The epigraph to this chapter illustrates one way of indicating an interrupted exit. Troilus commands his army to march offstage. The rhyming words reinforce the impression that the scene has come to an end. Then the speaker assertively halts the movement, and a new, unexpected dramatic action begins: Troilus turns to address the distant tents of the Greek army. After he speaks seven lines of threatening rhetoric, the audience is prepared once again to watch the actors leave the stage. We hear another command for an exit and another rhyming couplet, but once again the movement is interrupted:

> Strike a free march to Troy, with comfort goe:
> Hope of revenge, shall hide our inward woe.
> *Enter Pandarus.*
> *Pand.* But heare you? heare you?
> *Troy.* Hence broker, lackie, ignomy, and shame
> Pursue thy life, and live aye with thy name. *Exeunt.*
> *Pan.* A goodly medcine for mine aking bones;
> [Folio, 3566-71; 5.10.30-35]

In this instance, a new voice is the cause of the second interrupted exit, but the pattern is basically the same. Expectations are built up through a combination of clearly understandable commands and theatrical conventions such as rhymes and drumbeats for a march. Then the expectations are frustrated.

It has been suggested that various practical considerations led playwrights of both medieval and Renaissance English drama to incorporate many instructions for entrances and exits within the actors' dialogue.[1] Whatever the origin, playwrights exploited the possibilities inherent in the need to signal or to forewarn their actors' movements into and out of the playing space. A variation of the same dramatic "figure" may be found, for example, in the Wakefield Master's *Second Shepherds' Play*. The three shepherds leave the playing area designated as Mak's house after they fail to discover their stolen sheep, disguised as a swaddled infant. The first shepherd abruptly recalls that they did not leave a gift for the newborn "child," and so they pause while the youngest retraces his steps to Mak's door. The impulse to interrupt their movement back toward their "flocks" and away from the playing area at Mak's house results in finding the sheep. The plot of the scene then unfolds in a direction contrary to the expectation that was established as the shepherds first began to move away.[2]

Despite its widespread use by playwrights, the interrupted exit is mentioned in only one out of the many discussions of medieval, Renaissance, and Shakespearean staging I have examined.[3] This valuable "figure" of dramatic dialogue occurs repeatedly in Shakespeare's plays. Sometimes it is used for comic effects, as a character is repeatedly urged to hurry away but then is called back again. Sometimes the same scheme of words and movements is used to indicate the psychological turmoil of a character issuing commands. And sometimes the interrupted exit is used as a significant turning point for the reversal of an expected development in a plot. The first half of this chapter will demonstrate the uses of interrupted exits in *King Lear*, both in passages that are the same in the two early texts and in several that are in variant forms. The latter half of the chapter explores the textual crux in Kent's long address to the Gentleman in 3.1, demonstrating that, within the context of two interrupted exits, an interrupted speech added in the Folio text changes the "shape" of the scene as well as the ways in which the scene handles issues of plot and characterization.

Two types of interrupted exits appear in *King Lear*. The simpler variety serves as a kind of theatrical punctuation or rhetorical device useful for setting off part of a speech in isolation from what went before. For example, Regan dismisses Oswald at the end of 4.5, but then speaks another sentence to him concerning a different subject:

> If you do finde him [i.e., Edmund], pray you give him this;
> And when your Mistris heares thus much from you,
> I pray desire her call her wisedome to her.
> So fare you well:
> If you do chance to heare of that blinde Traitor,
> Preferment fals on him, that cuts him off.
>   *Stew*. Would I could meet Madam, I should shew
> What party I do follow.
>   *Reg*. Fare thee well.   *Exeunt*
>   [Folio, 2420-28; 4.5.33-40; similarly Quarto, I2]

The initial impulse toward the exit is given when Regan says, "So fare you well." Then Regan's afterthought about Gloucester suspends the movement for the space of three and a half lines; and the delayed exit is then concluded when she says, "Fare thee well."

Another interrupted exit of this pattern is found in Edmund's speech to his brother at the end of 1.2. In that speech, the idea for the exit is first established with words and action, "Pray ye goe, there's my key," and then a belated thought introduces a delaying conversation, "if you do stirre abroad, goe arm'd." After five lines of dialogue, the movement is resumed and the exit is completed.

Another relatively simple instance of an interrupted exit appears as a possibility in 1.4 as Oswald is driven from the stage by Kent.

> *Ste.* Ile not be strucken my Lord.
> *Kent.* Nor tript neither, you base Foot-ball plaier.
> *Lear.* I thanke thee fellow.
> Thou serv'st me, and Ile love thee.
> *Kent.* Come sir, **arise, away,** Ile teach you differences: away, away, if you will measure your lubbers length againe, tarry, but away, **goe too,** have you wisedome, **so.**
> [Folio, 615-21; 1.4.85-92; boldface indicates material only in Folio]

A director may have Kent kick Oswald's feet out from under him after Oswald's line, "Ile not be strucken my Lord," raise Oswald up and push him toward an exit at "Come sir, arise, away," trip him once again at "if you will measure your lubbers length againe, tarry," and finally allow him to depart at "but away, goe too, have you wisedome, so." Several words in Kent's last speech quoted above appear only in the Folio text; "arise, away" on line 619, and "goe too" and "so" on line 621. It is not clear if they signal additional knockdowns or if they simply provide breathing space while the actors set themselves up for this display of dramatic tumbling. The basic structure of the interrupted exit is, however, the same in both the Quarto and the Folio.

In the examples discussed above, despite their local dramatic interest, the interrupted exits are relatively minor components of the total action of the scenes in which they appear. In contrast, a more complex type of interrupted exit in *Lear* forms the basic structure of important dramatic passages. Lear's interruption of the exit of France and Cordelia in 1.1,

Oswald's interruption of the exit of Edgar and Gloucester in 4.6, and Edgar's interruption of Albany's exit in 5.1 serve as critical turning points of the play. These are carefully plotted junctions of expectation and surprise.

For an interrupted exit that is to be a major shifting in the plot, the preparation is as important to dramatic success as the moment of the surprise itself. A pattern of expectation must be established before a reversal has any dramatic effect. The elaborate banishment of Kent in 1.1 offers a precedent on which the audience can base its idea of how Cordelia will leave the stage, although the realization of Cordelia's exit is quite different.

We are prepared for Kent's exit in 1.1 by three commands from Lear, the first two of which seem to have little effect on Kent:

Lear. Peace Kent,
Come not betweene the Dragon and his wrath,
I lov'd her most, and thought to set my rest
On her kind nursery. Hence and avoid my sight:

Kent. My life I never held but as pawne
To wage against thine enemies, nere feare to loose it,
Thy safety being motive.
   Lear. Out of my sight.

   Lea. Heare me recreant, . . .
. . . if on the tenth day following,
Thy banisht trunke be found in our Dominions,
The moment is thy death, away. By Jupiter,
This shall not be revok'd,
                [Folio, 129-32, 166-69, 181-93;
                    1.1.121-24, 155-57, 166-79]

Kent's speech following the last of the three quoted above is a ceremonious farewell. Each couplet is aimed at a specific audience, and each strikes directly, memorably, and painfully:

Fare thee well King, sith thus thou wilt appeare,
Freedome lives hence, and banishment is here;
The Gods to their deere shelter take thee Maid,
That justly think'st, and hast most rightly said:

And your large speeches, may your deeds approve,
That good effects may spring from words of love:
Thus Kent, O Princes, bids you all adew,
Hee'l shape his old course, in a Country new. *Exit.*
[Folio, 194-201; 1.1.180-87]

These sententious, strongly end-stopped, and rhymed lines give an unmistakable formality to the occasion.

The same kinds of signals preparatory to a mannered leave-taking precede Cordelia's apparent moment of departure. For seventy lines, the dialogue has been concerned with the conditions under which Cordelia will leave Lear's court. Lear sets the terms for her departure almost as unequivocally as he did for Kent's:

Will you with those infirmities she owes,
Unfriended, new adopted to our hate,
Dow'rd with our curse, and stranger'd with our oath,
Take her or, leave her.
[Folio, 221-24; 1.1.201-5]

The King of France takes up Cordelia's hand (on either the third or fourth lines of the speech quoted below) and prepares her, the King and court, and the audience for another ceremonial exit. The sententiousness and the end-stopped rhymes, which begin after he "seizes upon" Cordelia, recall the sense and the sound of Kent's exit earlier in the scene:

Fairest Cordelia, that art most rich being poore,
Most choise forsaken, and most lov'd despis'd,
Thee and thy vertues here I seize upon,
Be it lawfull I take up what's cast away.
Gods, Gods! 'Tis strange, that from their cold'st neglect
My Love should kindle to enflam'd respect.
Thy dowrelesse Daughter King, throwne to my chance,
Is Queene of us, of ours, and our faire France:
Not all the Dukes of watrish Burgundy,
Can buy this unpriz'd precious Maid of me.
Bid them farewell Cordelia, though unkinde,
Thou loosest here a better where to finde.
[Folio, 275-86; 1.1.250-61]

During the last couplet, France seems to advance Cordelia so that she may make her own farewell speech to Lear and the court.

But just as Cordelia disturbed the ceremonial distribution of the kingdom, and as Kent broke into Lear's mannered dispossession of Cordelia, so Lear disrupts the formally patterned plan of Cordelia's exit. Rather than the expected speech and the formal withdrawal of France and Cordelia, the audience hears Lear himself speak and then sees him depart, taking with him most of the courtiers and attendants:

> Thou hast her France, let her be thine, for we
> Have no such Daughter, nor shall ever see
> That face of hers againe, therfore be gone,
> Without our Grace, our Love, our Benizon:
> Come Noble Burgundie. *Flourish.*   *Exeunt.*
>
>   [Folio, 287-91; 1.1.262-66]

Although this is the third disruption of ceremonial order in the scene, after first Cordelia and then Kent have interfered with Lear's plans, it still surprises an audience because the unfulfilled expectations about Cordelia's exit have been so carefully prepared.

The figure of the interrupted exit immediately appears twice again as Cordelia makes ready to resume her departure with France. France prompts her again to speak, and she addresses her sisters with a valediction ending in a rhyming couplet and an exit tag line:

>   *Fra.* Bid farwell to your Sisters.
>   *Cor.* The Jewels of our Father, with wash'd eies
> Cordelia leaves you, I know you what you are,
> And like a Sister am most loth to call
> Your faults as they are named. Love well our Father:
> To your professed bosomes I commit him,
> But yet alas, stood I within his Grace,
> I would prefer him to a better place;
> So farewell to you both.
>
>   [Folio, 292-300; 1.1.267-75]

Regan and Goneril delay Cordelia's exit once again, however, and Goneril's rhyme in the passage below, "scanted-wanted," suggests that this couplet also signals the beginning of a move or a turn toward an exit, as if Goneril now intends to spurn Cordelia and France just as her father did:

> *Regn.* Prescribe not us our dutie.
> *Gon.* Let your study
> Be to content your Lord, who hath receiv'd you
> At Fortunes almes, you have obedience scanted,
> And well are worth the want that you have wanted.
> [Folio, 301-5; 1.1.276-79]

The exchange of closing or departing couplets ends with a final speech by Cordelia, twenty lines after the specific idea for the exit was first introduced and interrupted:

> *Cor.* Time shall unfold what plighted cunning hides,
> Who covers faults, at last with shame derides:
> Well may you prosper.
> *Fra.* Come my faire Cordelia. *Exit France and Cor.*
> [Folio, 306-9; 1.1.280-82]

Lear's speech beginning "Thou hast her France" first interrupted this exit, then Regan's short remark, "Prescribe not us our dutie," delayed the move again, and finally Cordelia halted a possible exit move by Goneril with her couplet beginning "Time shall unfold." Through language and visible display, these interrupted exits reveal the steadfastness of Cordelia and France as they wait to withdraw, the self-righteous anger of Regan and Goneril, and the fierce indignation of King Lear. Only when seen or imagined in a theatrical context of expectation, surprise, delay, and resolution do the fine details of the script spring to life and appear meaningful.

A second extended action centered on an interrupted exit produces surprising changes in the behavior of both Edgar and Gloucester near the end of 4.6, after Oswald discovers them on the heath. As with the interrupted exits in 1.1, the Quarto and the Folio offer substantially the same text for this passage. The interrupted exit and its consequences take up the last of the three sections of 4.6. The first part of the scene shows Edgar's artificial miracle, the purpose of which is to restore in Gloucester the will to live despite his pain and disappointment. Initially Edgar meets with success. His father responds to the bizarre treatment with surprising strength:

> *Glou.* I do remember now: henceforth Ile beare
> Affliction, till it do cry out it selfe
> Enough, enough, and dye.
> [Folio, 2520-22; 4.6.75-77]

The second section of this scene begins at Lear's entrance, two lines after those quoted above. The dialogue in this section reduces Gloucester to helpless tears, so pitiable a sight that Lear himself tries to comfort his suffering friend:

> *Lear.* If thou wilt weepe my Fortunes, take my eyes.
> I know thee well enough, thy name is Glouster:
> Thou must be patient; we came crying hither:
> Thou know'st, the first time that we smell the Ayre
> We wawle, and cry.
> [Folio, 2618-21; 4.6.176-80]

After Lear runs off, Gloucester still maintains enough strength to reject suicide, and in the dialogue quoted below he seems to draw vitality from the simple touch of his son's hand.

> *Glou.* You ever gentle Gods, take my breath from me,
> Let not my worser Spirit tempt me againe
> To dye before you please.
> *Edg.* Well pray you Father.
> *Glou.* Now good sir, what are you?
> *Edg.* A most poore man, made tame to Fortunes blows
> Who, by the Art of knowne, and feeling sorrowes,
> Am pregnant to good pitty. Give me your hand,
> Ile leade you to some biding.
> *Glou.* Heartie thankes:
> The bountie, and the benizon of Heaven
> To boot, and boot.
> [Folio, 2663-74; 4.6.217-26]

This is the end of the second major part of the scene. At this point the plot seems to be working toward a restorative ending. Edgar calls his father "Father," raising the audience's hope that perhaps he will reveal his identity; Gloucester expresses an interest in the qualities of his benefactor, also raising the possibility that Edgar may be recognized; and when he joins hands with Edgar, Gloucester speaks with an alliterative liveliness that indicates revived spirits.

In the final segment of 4.6, the image of concord with its promise of restoration and its graceful conjunction of Gloucester's parental need and Edgar's filial service is destroyed by Oswald's interruption of their exit:

> *Enter Steward.*
> *Stew.* A proclaim'd prize: most happie
> That eyelesse head of thine, was first fram'd flesh
> To raise my fortunes. Thou old, unhappy Traitor,
> Breefely thy selfe remember: the Sword is out
> That must destroy thee.
> [Folio, 2675-80; 4.6.226-30]

As with other crucial interrupted exits, the plot develops in new and unexpected directions after the initial movement is stopped.

Although Edgar successfully defends Gloucester and slays Oswald, the fight diverts his mind away from his father and toward the larger society of the play. His attention is so occupied that he stops responding to what Gloucester says, a sharp departure from the sensitive concentration the audience observed in the opening part of the scene. Edgar addresses himself to Oswald's corpse, then speaks inattentively to Gloucester, and then returns to the corpse:

> *Edg.* I know thee well. A serviceable Villaine,
> As duteous to the vices of thy Mistris,
> As badnesse would desire.
> *Glou.* What, is he dead?
> *Edg.* Sit you downe Father: rest you.
> Let's see these Pockets; the letters that he speakes of
> May be my Friends: hee's dead; I am onely sorry
> He had no other Deathsman. Let us see:
> [Folio, 2704-11; 4.6.252-58]

To Gloucester's question, "What, is he dead?" Edgar doesn't reply at once. Instead, distracted, he places his father aside.

(Indeed, it seems likely that Edgar's words, "hee's dead; I am onely sorry . . . ," are not meant as responses to Gloucester but rather are Edgar's musings as he examines his fallen foe.) Edgar must then leave Gloucester alone onstage in order to drag Oswald's corpse off to burial.[4] He goes without a word to his father. Gloucester sinks into despondency. When Edgar returns, the exit that the two men began seventy lines earlier is once again resumed, but the circumstances are grimly altered. Gloucester wishes for madness as a relief from his "huge Sorrowes." Edgar, caught up in the excitement of intrigue and impending battle, seeks to "bestow" his father with a friend so that he might take up his new business. In appearance the original exit and the resumed exit are similar since in both Edgar reaches for Gloucester's hand. But earlier Edgar would have taken his father to "some biding," with connotations of peace and permanence, and later he says, "Ile bestow you," with connotations of temporary storage.

The design of this scene first establishes the expectation that Edgar and Gloucester will find "some biding," and then, through the use of an interrupted exit, the expectation is frustrated and the play moves forward toward its painful ending. The interrupted exit in 4.6 divides the moment when the father and child seem most restored to one another from the moment when destructive forces impose terrible conditions on that restoration. For Lear and Cordelia in the main plot of the play, an equivalent of this crisis seems to occur between the end of 4.7 and the beginning of 5.1. Lear and Cordelia, restored to one other, go out together, but their exit (in the Folio text) is immediately followed by the entrance of Edmund and Regan at the head of an army threatening the peaceful reconciliation. Instead of withdrawing to safety after being reconciled (at least partially) with their fathers, both Edgar and Cordelia are swept up into battle. In the brief prelude to the battle (5.2), they are both shown to the audience leading their helpless fathers by the hand, the promise or hope of peace exposed to the hazards of war. This painful twisting of our expectations begins with the interrupted exit in 4.6.

Another important interrupted exit works in a similarly complex manner in 5.1, when Edgar momentarily stops Albany. The Duke is leaving to prepare for the battle against the forces of France and rebel Englishmen. This crucial exchange will be discussed in the next chapter, which deals with variants in the characterization of Albany.

Two more interrupted exits in *King Lear*, found in 3.1, form part of a complicated series of variants that have been the subject of confused commentary by textual and literary critics for over 250 years. Three closely related but distinct aspects of the play receive different treatments in the Quarto, the Folio, and the modern composite versions of the scene. First, the three versions offer three different plans for the dramatic action of the latter part of the dialogue between Kent and the unnamed Gentleman. Second, the three texts offer different reasons for the French "invasion" of Britain, a crucial topic that is the focus of at least three other major variants later in the play. Third, the three texts each offer different versions of the dramatic relationship between Kent and the Gentleman, alternatives created by changed levels of diction and rhetoric. Characterization, stage movement, and narrative plotting are each affected by the variants. The poetic and dramatic compression found in the different versions of the passage demands an extended discussion because the events in the scene are quick and subtle.

The textual variant that produces the crucial problems occurs in Kent's long speech in the scene. In the Quarto text, Kent has five orderly sentences, quoted below with numbers inserted at the beginnning of each sentence for the purpose of this analysis:

[1] Sir I doe know you,
And dare upon the warrant of my Arte,
Commend a deare thing to you, [2] there is division,
Although as yet the face of it be cover'd,
With mutuall cunning, twixt Albany and Cornwall
[3] But true it is, from France there comes a power
Into this scattered kingdome, who alreadie wise in our
 negligence,
Have secret feet in some of our best Ports,
And are at point to shew their open banner.
[4] Now to you, if on my credit you dare build so farre,

> To make your speed to Dover, you shall find
> Some that will thanke you, making just report
> Of how unnaturall and bemadding sorrow
> The King hath cause to plaine,
> [5] I am a Gentleman of blood and breeding,
> And from some knowledge and assurance,
> Offer this office to you.
> [Quarto, F3^v; 3.1.17-42]

In the first sentence, Kent says that his trust in the Gentleman permits him to convey "a deare thing," or valuable news to him. The second sentence reports news of hidden dissension in England. The third, beginning the part of the speech unique to the Quarto, tells more secret news of French armies landing or about to land in English ports in order to take advantage of known English weakness. In the fourth sentence, Kent invites or instructs the Gentleman to travel to Dover with the news of Lear's unnatural treatment by his daughters. In the final sentence, Kent attempts to establish himself as a person of social stature, and therefore worthy of trust. Thus there are four clearly distinguished actions in this speech. Kent (1) announces his trust in the Gentleman, (2) relays his secret news, (3) urges the Gentleman to go to Dover, and (4) asserts his own honesty.

The Gentleman's reply to Kent's speech, and Kent's reaction to the Gentleman's response are verbally the same in the Quarto and the Folio:

> *Gent.* I will talke further [**farther** in Quarto] with you.
> *Kent.* No, do not:
> For confirmation that I am much more
> Then my out-wall; open this Purse, and take
> What it containes. If you shall see Cordelia,
> (As feare not but you shall) shew her this Ring,
> And she will tell you who that Fellow is
> That yet you do not know.
> [Folio, 1639-46; 3.1.43-49]

To make sense out of Kent's otherwise inexplicable objection, "No, do not," it is necessary to recognize that the Gentleman's line, "I will talke further with you," is a conventional code for breaking off a conversation, not for continuing. (See, for example, *Macbeth*, 1.5.71, as Macbeth avoids committing himself to his wife's plan, saying "We will speak further." Also, in the first scene of *Lear*, Regan similarly signals that she is ending her conference with Goneril: "We shall further thinke of it.") So, after Kent's long speech the Gentleman tries to end the scene. Kent prevents the exit, however, with his urgent appeal, "No, do not." Then he offers a purse with evidence he hopes will demonstrate that he is not merely a rough servant. The dialogue and the stage movement implied by it are in the form of an interrupted exit. The Gentleman in the Quarto version listens to Kent's news, hears out his offer about Dover, and allows Kent to attest to his "blood and breeding." Then he decides to put Kent off, probably turns to leave, and Kent stops him.

Kent's long speech has a different form in the Folio text, and the Gentleman's response, although superficially similar, signals a somewhat different dramatic action. Only two complete sentences appear in the Folio, along with part of a third, which Kent never concludes. Once again, numbers are inserted at the beginning of each sentence in the following passage. The part unique to the Folio begins after the fifth line:

[1] Sir, I do know you,
And dare upon the warrant of my note
Commend a deere thing to you. [2] There is division
(Although as yet the face of it is cover'd
With mutuall cunning) 'twixt Albany, and Cornwall:
Who have, as who have not, that their great Starres
Thron'd and set high; Servants, who seeme no lesse,
Which are to France the Spies and Speculations
Intelligent of our State. [3] What hath bin seene,
Either in snuffes, and packings of the Dukes,
Or the hard Reine which both of them hath borne
Against the old kinde King; or something deeper,
Whereof (perchance) these are but furnishings.[5]
Gent. I will talke further with you.
[Folio, 1626-39; 3.1.17-42]

Here Kent gets through the entirety of only the first of the four actions he completes in the Quarto version of this speech. He states his trust in the Gentleman. Then, as in the Quarto, he begins to talk about political trouble in England. The secret news that he is ready to impart occupies the remainder of the lines in this speech. But Kent fails to reach the predicate verb of the second sentence of news (the third sentence of the speech) before he is cut off. In the Folio text the Gentleman interrupts Kent's speech abruptly at "these are but furnishings," a sharp contrast to the complete hearing he gives to the version of Kent's speech found in the Quarto. The Gentleman's reply uses practically the same words, but because he forcefully interrupts Kent's speech in the Folio he means "I will not listen to anything else you say," rather than "I will not respond to your proposal," his meaning in the Quarto. In the Folio version of this speech, the Gentleman rejects Kent himself, not Kent's proposal. Kent's next speech, in which he prevents the Gentleman's departure, is of necessity more forceful in the Folio than in its verbally identical Quarto counterpart since it must overcome a much stronger rejection.

The dramatic use of this interrupted speech is completely consistent with Shakespeare's continuing practice from his earliest plays to his latest. Instead of grammatical completeness, the Folio has a more obvious dramatic conflict at the end of Kent's speech as the Gentleman interrupts him. Similar curtailing of sentences for the sake of vigorous dialogue abound in *King Lear*. If the passage is considered as a script to be performed rather than as a poem or a story to be read, then the Folio version of this dramatic moment is not without real theatrical strength.

In modern editions a clumsy composite version of Kent's speech results from grafting the lines unique to the Quarto onto the end of the Folio version. The alternative endings from the two early texts do not flow smoothly where they are joined.

> ... What hath been seen,
> Either in snuffs and packings of the Dukes,
> Or the hard rein which both of them hath borne
> Against the old kind King; or something deeper,

Whereof (perchance) these are but furnishings—
[But, true it is, from France there comes a power . . .
    [Riverside edition, 3.1.25-30]

Modern editors suggest, following Capell, that lines were lost between "furnishings" and "But, true it is." Kenneth Muir, the New Arden editor, proposes that the gap between the two component parts of the speech was planned by Shakespeare. However, it should be noted that Shakespeare generally uses this rhetorical figure, *aposiopesis* (the breaking off of a sentence in the midst of a speech), only for occasions of emotional intensity. The transition between the two sections of Kent's speech is more a bibliographical quirk than a dramatic subtlety. The dramatically justified speech interruption in the Folio text becomes an unmotivated and suspicious lacuna in the composite version.

The composite version becomes the longest speech in the play, about 25 percent longer than Edmund's soliloquy at the beginning of 1.2. The delivery of such a lengthy passage in the midst of a play notable for its rapid pace would require careful preparation by the performer in order to keep the scene from losing the feeling of being a brief pause during an urgent search on a stormy night. The Quarto and, to a greater extent, the Folio maintain the feeling of urgency by the rapid sequence of actions within Kent's speech and in the exchange that follows it. The composite version seems instead to suspend the action during Kent's now sixteen-line report of the secret news. Then the pace must be accelerated again. Of the three texts, the Folio provides the most energetic action, while the composite is the most discursive and relaxed.

Not directly affected by the interrupted exits, the second aspect of the different texts is their variant presentation of the important issue of the French army and the reasons for the French invasion. The information reported in the variant lines rather than the actions they imply are the concern here. Neither the Quarto nor the Folio may be considered "incomplete," "inadequate," or "clumsy," but the composite version in fact introduces difficulties not found in either early text.

The French are secretly invading, Kent tells the Gentleman

in the third sentence of his long Quarto speech, because they know that the English dukes are preoccupied with their own contention and are negligent in defending the realm against foreign incursion. In the Quarto text the French are unaware of the "unnaturall and bemadding sorrow" inflicted on Lear. This news is the reason for the Gentleman's errand to Dover (Sentence 4 of Kent's speech). The later passages in the Quarto, particularly in 4.3, which refer to the French forces seem designed to overcome an initial impression created by Kent's speech that the French are engaged in an opportunistic adventure. It must be stressed that the expedition of the French in the Quarto text is unrelated to Lear's plight, of which they have no knowledge prior to their landing. According to this text, Kent implies that the Gentleman's report would go far to legitimize the French invasion; it might also bring Englishmen to fight alongside the French against the dukes.

In contrast, the Folio version of Kent's speech does not report that the French are present on English soil at all. Instead, Kent says that the French king's spies, and by implication the king himself, are fully aware not only of the division between Albany and Cornwall, but also of "the hard Reine which both of them hath borne / Against the old kind King." Kent does not send the Gentleman toward Dover for two reasons. First, in the Folio version the French are not sending an army, nor has Dover been identified as a rallying point for friends of King Lear. Second, the French already know of Lear's mistreatment from their own "spies and speculations" in the households of Albany and Cornwall.

Dr. Johnson suggested that the variant here was introduced because "Shakespeare thought his plot opened rather too early, and made the alteration to veil the event [the French landing] from the audience" (*Works of Shakespeare*, VI, 79). Later references to the French force in England, as well as several small changes in the Folio text tend to support Johnson's speculation.[6] The first mention in the Folio text of any force gathered to defend Lear or to oppose Albany and Cornwall is found in 3.3, where Gloucester confides the news to Edmund. The Quarto version of this passage simply reaffirms the news of French landings already announced by Kent in 3.1 in the Quarto version:

> *Glost.* . . . these injuries
> The King now beares, will be revenged home
> Ther's part of a power already landed,
> [Quarto, G; 3.3.11-13]

However, in the Folio version of Gloucester's speech this is not a power "landed," but rather "footed." Consistent with the Folio text of 3.1, there is no connotation of invasion at this point in the Folio. Rebellion is suggested instead. Indeed, in the Folio the only announcements of a French force or a foreign army in England are Cornwall's statement at the opening of 3.7, "the Army of France is landed," and Oswald's line referring to Albany at the beginning of 4.2: "I told him of the Army that was landed." Previous references to the nationality of armed friends of King Lear are extremely and, I feel, purposefully vague in the Folio, especially in the absence of remarks about the French army in 3.1. Thus, all mention of the military intervention by France in England is put off until approximately four hundred lines later in the Folio than in the Quarto. This delay creates no problem in plotting and no confusion. To the contrary, it adds another note of surprise for the audience, a change consonant with other variants creating unexpected events found in the Folio text.

The composite version of this passage presents the issue of the French invasion in yet another light. In the modern text the spies in the households of Albany and Cornwall, Kent reports, gave France the news of contention between the dukes, of their mistreatment of King Lear, and of the unprepared defenses of the country. On the basis of this news, an army was brought secretly to England. The Gentleman, Kent continues, should hurry to Dover with news of Lear's recent suffering.

Just as the modern text seems to create a lacuna in the midst of Kent's first long speech, it also seems to present an odd flaw in Kent's reasoning. The French already know of Lear's troubles with the dukes. Reports from their own spies on this subject were a major reason for their intervention.

Spies in the households of the dukes would also be able to relay the latest details of their acts against Lear. If this is the case, there seems to be no need for the Gentleman to leave Lear after he may be found in the storm and then speed toward Dover with news already in the possession of Lear's friends. To restate the problem in its simplest terms, in the Folio France has the news and Kent need not and does not send the Gentleman to Dover; in the Quarto France could use the news, so the Gentleman is urged to speed toward Dover; in the composite version France has the news *and* the Gentleman is sent to Dover with the same news.

The composite text has been defended for 250 years on the grounds that all its information was "necessary" to the plot. This is simply not true. The concept of dramatic necessity is a valid one, but the necessity of an individual passage must be tested rather than simply declared. If subsequent dramatic events become confused or seem irrational or haphazard as a consequence of omitting a passage, then that passage may be considered necessary. Kent's soliloquy when he assumes his lowly disguise in 1.4, for example, is by this standard necessary to the play. The facts and the actions in the composite version of Kent's long speech in 3.1 fail this test; some are even superfluous. The composite text presents too much information to justify the mission to Dover proposed by Kent to the Gentleman. It makes little sense for Kent to send the Gentleman to Dover with a redundant report of news when the man might aid in rescuing and protecting Lear in the storm at hand. This problem exists only in the composite text. In summary, the Quarto version of this passage raises questions about the motives of the French invasion; the Gentleman's errand to Dover, which is only in the Quarto version, seems part of the Quarto's solution to the problem of motives. The Folio version eliminates the problem entirely by offering a different version of Kent's speech and by changing later references about the opposing force from a "landed" to a "footed" army. The composite text creates a new problem of justifying the Gentleman's dispatch to Dover.

Analysis of the variant uses of language in the Quarto and Folio versions of Kent's speech reveals important changes in the dramatic relationship established between the two men. These changes are related directly to the interrupted speech in the Folio. In the Quarto text, Kent tries to win the Gentleman's trust by a show of honesty, a sharing of secrets, and a forthright claim of "gentle" status. His sentences are relatively simple. The intention of each remark is quite clear; the Gentleman certainly is able to comprehend exactly what Kent is asking of him. The Gentleman's rejection of Kent's offer, signified by his line, "I will talke farther with you," follows from a complete hearing of Kent's proposal and his claims of authority. Kent's next speech, in its Quarto context, is more successful than his first in winning the Gentleman's confidence simply because it presents more tangible and convincing evidences of Kent's reliability. The literary style of the second speech is no different from that of the first.

The Folio variant of this passage creates an inordinately complex first speech for Kent.[7] (Perhaps the only utterances in the play that can match these lines for courtliness and obscurity are the involuted speeches addressed by Goneril to Lear when she threatens to censure him in 1.4.) This style of speech seems particularly inappropriate to Kent's servile station. Also, his remarks about spies in the courts should, in the eyes of the Gentleman, draw suspicion upon Kent himself as a possible French agent. After all, Kent is a new man who has appeared out of nowhere to join Lear's train, a provocative roughneck who has managed first to offend Goneril, and then so to incense Regan and Cornwall in the course of simply delivering a letter that they left him sitting overnight in the stocks. When (following the Folio text) this gruff fellow suddenly begins speaking of state secrets in a rhetorical style alien to his habit, the Gentleman quite reasonably distrusts the medium even before he hears the full message. The Gentleman's rejection of Kent must be based more on Kent's mannered language than any other factor, because he hears little of Kent's matter. Kent's next speech, only in its Folio context, suddenly drops from polysyllabic and complicated obscurity down to plain words in clear syntax. In contrast, both of Kent's speeches are simple in the Quarto, and the modern composite version buries the stylistic shift within the two pieces of Kent's elongated speech. The Folio's change in style adds another "dimension" to the dramatic exchange. The Folio consequently makes more believable the Gentleman's shift from suspicious rejection, "I will talke further with you," to friendly concern, "Give me your hand, / Have you no more to say?"

This Folio variant in Kent's style, which first motivates an interruption and then heightens the dramatic surprise of the subsequent action, either has not been noticed or has been misunderstood by modern critics, undoubtedly because the conflated version of Kent's first speech makes invisible the important contextual contrast between Kent's two speeches in the Folio. For example, in a valuable discussion of language and style in *King Lear*, Sheldon P. Zitner remarks that in this play most "courtly speeches are only superficially appropriate to their speaker's station. The decorum of the high or court style, then, is undercut in a variety of ways. . . . It is at best with Kent a brief convenience—a cachet to undo the impression of his dress and situation when he encounters a gentleman ally."[8] Reliance upon a reputable composite text prevents this critic from seeing that (1) the Quarto version lacks any high or court style in Kent's speech, and (2) distrust rather than acceptance result from the courtly lines added in the Folio. When Kent uses courtly speech to approach the Gentleman on an equal footing, he actually drives the Gentleman away. The Folio text in fact reinforces this critic's basic premise that a "surface of court rhetoric becomes a bitter irony" (p. 6). The modern composite text misleads Zitner. Only in the modern version does the high style in Kent's speech appear as an exception to its otherwise ironic dramatic usage.

The composite text reduces the display of dramatic tension between Kent and the Gentleman at the moment when the Gentleman first turns away, saying "I will talk further. . . ." The modern text eliminates the Gentleman's interruption of Kent's speech found in the Folio. It reduces the urgency or even the need for the Gentleman's errand to Dover, so important in the Quarto. It extends the length of time that the Gentleman stands in the rain listening to Kent. For these reasons, in this version the Gentleman's initial rejection of Kent's offer does not imply much if any distrust of Kent. Such is the reading of the composite text of the scene given by Rosalie L. Colie, who finds the exchange of dialogue in this scene one of the play's inexplicable passages: "Nor do we know why the Gentleman . . . so readily trusts Kent on the heath; simply, we must accept that two good-hearted people, devoted to the king and Cordelia, trust one another on sight and do each other's offices readily for that trust."[9] Apparently it is the lack of dramatic point or purpose in the modern version which leads other critics to agree with Colie in finding this passage anomalous or simply "bad." Emrys Jones, for example, comments that this part of the scene, "about the growing division between the Dukes and the arrival of the French 'power' is very clumsily inserted." Alice Walker calls the passage from the Folio version, and thus the conflation which includes it, "dramatically unnecessary." E. K. Chambers and Madeleine Doran find that the Folio and the composite versions probably resulted from the interference of a censor and, perhaps, subsequent hasty or ill-considered patching.[10] These speculations about and judgments of the passage indicate an inadequate appreciation of the dramatic design of the Folio version or, more likely, a failure to notice that the Folio version indeed possesses a dramatic design.

What, finally, is the purpose of this scene? Is it enhanced in the Folio version's more sharply drawn interrupted exits? First, the scene as a whole serves to introduce the convention of action out on the heath. Except for Edgar's solo scene when he plans his disguise as Poor Tom in 2.3, all previous dramatic action must be imagined as taking place indoors or within courtyard enclosures. For the first time the pastoral, or what has also been called the antipastoral, environment of the latter half of the play is shown to the audience by the sound effects of wind and thunder, and by the words and mimed action of Kent and the Gentleman as they protect themselves from the "storm."[11] Second, the beginning of the scene establishes a kind of expectation or ad hoc convention about the likelihood of chance meetings in a supposedly wild area of ill-defined expanse. The audience is led to imagine a search that preceded the moment of meeting and another which follows, both being of some indeterminate duration.

Finally, the interrupted exits in 3.1 also arouse expectations in the audience concerning the consequences of these chance meetings on the heath in the storm. At the moment of the first interrupted exit, particularly in the Folio, it appears to the audience that the two men may part from one another estranged. But after the second interrupted exit, when the Gentleman stops Kent to grasp his hand, they have clearly joined in a common purpose. A hint, nothing more than a suggestion, is given in this first scene in the pastoral wilds that men may find out friends here. The actions implied by the interrupted exits show that trust may not be earned easily. The handshake between Kent and the Gentleman at the end of this scene is one of the first hopeful, integrative signs in the play since France took Cordelia by the hand in the first scene. I believe that later scenes build upon the audience's expectation, established in 3.1, that such meetings might indeed lead to a happy resolution of *King Lear*. Of course, these expectations will be frustrated. The poignancy of the frustration, however, depends to a large measure upon how "real" is the possibility of success. In the Quarto, Kent's news of the French army already in England establishes the hope of success; the exchange of faith between the two men seems of secondary importance. But the Folio version, with no reference to the French force, creates a real feeling of potential restoration only through its more vividly designed interrupted actions.

This examination of the three versions of 3.1 yields the following conclusions: the Folio text represents a careful revision of the Quarto version, affecting the local dramatic action, the overall plot, the relationships between characters, and the meaning of the scene in the greater context of the play. The modern composite version diminishes the intensity of the action within the scene, confuses the plot line that relates the involvement of France in England, makes trivial the relationship between Kent and the Gentleman, and blurs the delicately indicated expectations concerning possible sources of aid for Lear.

Instead of providing a "good" text for readers, actors, and literary scholars, modern editors accidentally disguise the integrity of the two early versions of this passage. Although editors often mark with brackets the lines unique to the Quarto, these warnings have never been understood. During the past thirty years not one literary or dramatic analysis of this scene makes any reference to the original texts. The composite is read as if it were authoritative. Perhaps as a result of the growing respect for bibliographic and textual scholarship, nonspecialist readers trust what they are given. In this case, as in too many others in *King Lear*, the originals are more trustworthy.

Interrupted exits abound in *Lear*. The pattern seems ideal for the painful frustrations and broken expectations that give this play its awesome power. Although in appearance interrupted exits may differ markedly, the form is always the same. The major examples discussed in this chapter have very different scenic contexts: Lear breaks into the departure of France and Cordelia in the midst of a courtly pageant; Oswald stops Edgar and Gloucester on their way to refuge in the pastoral space near Dover; and Kent and the Gentleman delay one another's exits within the turmoil of wind and weather. But in each case Shakespeare first sets up a series of dramatic cues apparently leading to an exit move, and then he gives us an unexpected action to turn the play in a surprising direction.

CHAPTER V

The Role of Albany in the Quarto and Folio

> If we fling ourselves at the task, as Burbage and the rest had to do when he brought them a new manuscript, with something of the faith they must have had in him as a playwright, for all his disturbing genius—it may be we shall not do, so badly. But to this faith must be added something which the company from the Globe had also gained, a knowledge of his playwright's craft.
> Harley Granville-Barker, *Prefaces to Shakespeare,* II, xlv

The role of Albany in *King Lear* is a small one. The character appears in only five scenes and delivers altogether about fifty-five speeches. Nevertheless, variants in the Folio text related to this role raise crucial dramatic issues for readers and performers of the play.

Albany has attracted little attention from editors or from literary critics who comment on the play. G. I. Duthie mentions Albany only twice in his fifty-five-page introduction to the New [Cambridge] Shakespeare; Kenneth Muir mentions him once in the fifty pages of introductory material in the New Arden edition; and Alfred Harbage says not a word about Albany in his thirteen-page introduction to the Pelican edition.

Albany is thought of by critics as a good man in a difficult marital and political situation who carries himself honorably throughout the painful action of the play. The only question related to Albany that has aroused much critical discussion concerns the last speech of the final scene. In the Quarto text it is given to Albany, but in the Folio it is spoken instead by Edgar. Defenders of the Quarto ascription argue that since Albany is the highest-ranking nobleman alive at the end of the scene he should say the last words. (This convention is followed in each of the other major tragedies.) Most but by no means all twentieth-century editors, however, follow the Folio version. This choice is supported by the argument that Albany has abdicated his place in the kingdom, granting it to Kent and Edgar. Since Kent announces that he is at the point of death, Edgar is the new ruler of England and so he properly delivers the final speech.

Although this single variant is familiar to most Shakespeare scholars, almost no attention at all has been paid to the bibliographic complexity of the rest of Albany's part in the two early texts. Fully half of Albany's speeches are noticeably different in the two texts, variants occurring within the speeches themselves or in their immediate contexts. Additional significant changes appear in other character's lines referring to Albany when he is offstage. Finally, crucial alterations are made in passages that deal with themes or issues repeatedly involving Albany, particularly the conflicting themes of the need to fulfill social and familial obligations and the need to maintain civil order.

Act 1, Scene 1 to Act 5, Scene 1

The first major variant in the Folio text serves a double function. Lines only in the Folio identify the two dukes for the audience, and introduce a basic theme associated with both of them for the remainder of the play. The lines in boldface below appear only in the Folio:

> *Lear.* . . . and 'tis our fast intent,
> To shake all Cares and Businesse from our Age,
> Conferring them on yonger strengths, **while we
> Unburthen'd crawle toward death. Our son of Cornwal,
> And you our no lesse loving Sonne of Albany,
> We have this houre a constant will to publish
> Our daughters severall Dowers, that future strife
> May be prevented now.**
> [Folio, 43-50; 1.1.38-45]

Lear, in the Folio, expresses his concern about the need for preserving civil order by carefully binding his sons-in-law within the familial obligations implied by the dowries. Later in the same scene, the two dukes are given a brief but vivid action to play. Their speech in boldface below, only in the Folio, requires that Albany and Cornwall step forward when they restrain Lear in his rage against Kent:

> *Lear.* O Vassall! Miscreant.
> ***Alb. Cor.* Deare Sir forbeare.**
> *Kent.* Kill thy Physition,
>   [Folio, 175-77; 1.1.161-63]

This line, unique in F, TLN 176, offers a fleeting but clearly visible emblem.[1] Thirty lines earlier in the scene, Lear gave his authority and a crown to Albany and Cornwall. Here they move to assert their new power. Edmund later gives a suitable motto for this stage emblem when he reports that Edgar believes "Sonnes at perfect age, and Fathers declin'd, the Father should bee as Ward to the Son" (TLN 406-8; 1.2.72-73). In the Folio text, we see the sons-in-law act to constrain Lear. This is only a brief instant, but it foreshadows the developments of the rest of the play.

These two variants show how the themes of obligation and order appear more strongly in the Folio than in the Quarto, indicated by carefully pointed stage actions—first by Lear's courtly address singling out Albany and Cornwall, and then by the dukes' interposition at the moment of confrontation between Kent and Lear.

The next reference to Albany in the play is found in 1.4, when we see Lear discovering the strains incumbent upon his status as retired monarch in the household of his newly crowned children. In four separate passages, variants directly related to Albany again amplify the themes first raised in the opening scene, the obligation to the familial bond on the one hand and the desire to preserve civil peace on the other. The first variant identifies with greater precision in the Folio the manner in which the tension between Lear and his daughter's household is growing. The king is addressed by one of his hundred knights:

> My Lord, I know not what the matter is, but to my judgement your Highnesse is not entertain'd with that

Ceremonious affection as you were wont, theres a great abatement **of kindnesse** appeares as well in the generall dependants, as in the Duke himselfe also, and your Daughter.
[Folio, 586-91; 1.4.57-62;
boldface indicates material only in Folio]

That the abatement is one "of kindnesse" is only in the Folio, but both texts use the effects of repetition to implicate Albany as one of the offenders, "the Duke himselfe also." Lear's reply to his knight echoes the idea of "kindness":

... I have perceived a most faint neglect of late, which I have rather blamed as mine owne jealous curiositie, then as a very pretence and purpose of unkindnesse;
[Folio, 597-99; 1.4.68-71]

"Kindness" and "unkindness" are generally used to refer to all forms of family relationships, but Sir Thomas Elyot's *Boke Named the Governour*, thought to be a source for several important ideas in *King Lear*, offers a different gloss appropriate to Shakespeare's usage here and at later points in this play: "The moste damnable vice, and most agayne justice, in myne oppinion, is ingratitude, commenly called unkyndnesse.... He is unkynde, whiche denieth to have receyved any benefite that in dede he hathe receyved: ... He is moste unkynde that forgeteth."[2] Lear's knight charges Albany with no slight fault.

It must be noted that the audience has very little information about Albany upon which to base any opinion of him at this time in the play. Sophisticated readers who know about later actions in the play seem to discount or completely to ignore this early report of Albany's lapse from perfect "kindness." (Indeed, in Peter Mortenson's article, "The Role of Albany," *Shakespeare Quarterly*, 16 [1965], one of the few studies completely devoted to this character, this exchange between Lear and his knight passes unmentioned.) Shakespeare's dramatic characters are not always the same from the beginning to the end of a play. Albany's nature, in fact, is only gradually revealed to the audience. The Folio variants radically alter the pattern of his development. Confusion results from ignoring any step in the process.

A second variant related to Albany's part in 1.4 again shows the Duke attempting to restrain Lear in a moment of rage. Albany enters and observes the king acting wildly. Each of Lear's disconnected sentences, quoted below, is addressed to someone different: first to Goneril, then to Albany, then to his own servants, and then to the abstraction "Ingratitude." The audience sees Lear turning again and again:

> *Lear.* Woe, that too late repents:
> Is it your will, speake Sir? Prepare my Horses.
> Ingratitude! thou Marble-hearted Fiend,
> More hideous when thou shew'st thee in a Child,
> Then the Sea-monster.
>   ***Alb.* Pray Sir be patient.**
> *Lear.* Detested Kite, thou lyest.
> My Traine are men of choice, and rarest parts,
>   [Folio, 769-76; 1.4.257-63;
>   boldface indicates material only in Folio]

Albany's speech, only in the Folio, has little restraining effect, of course, but Albany's intent is still consonant with his speech in the first scene. He interrupts Lear's exclamation about Goneril's ingratitude in order to impose peace. The two themes are as clearly juxtaposed in the opposition between Albany and Lear as they are between Goneril and Lear when she demands that he curb his "riotous" knights. Albany's and Goneril's actions certainly differ in degree and in manner, but they both ask Lear to behave as they see fit.

In two later variants in this scene, the Folio text repeats the similar intents and the different tempers of the desires of Goneril and Albany to curb Lear. In his invariant speeches after his entrance, Albany cannot discern exactly why Lear is angry, raving, cursing, and gathering his company to leave the house. He does know Goneril provoked the king, but he shows only a weak attempt to protest the events that have clearly led to the alienation of his benefactor and father-in-law:

> *Lear.* . . . Thou shalt finde,
> That Ile resume the shape which thou dost thinke

> I have cast off for ever. *Exit*
> *Gon.* Do you marke that?
> *Alb.* I cannot be so partiall Gonerill,
> To the great love I beare you.
> *Gon.* Pray you content. What Oswald, hoa?
>   [Folio, 827-33; 1.4.308-13]

Albany's objection to Goneril's actions alienating her father is never spoken. Whatever he may have said, Goneril silences.

Albany's interrupted speech should not be interpreted as a strenuous effort by him on Lear's behalf, held in check only by Albany's great love for his wife. Strong objections to a course of action are raised by many characters on many different occasions in *King Lear*, such as Kent's attempt to advise Lear in the first scene, Gloucester's efforts to mitigate Cornwall's treatment of Kent in 2.2, or the Old Man's insistent desire to aid Gloucester in his blindness in 4.1. Albany's "resistance" to Goneril is certainly minimal by these standards.

The last variant in this group from 1.4 includes Albany's telling response to Goneril's declaration, in unmistakable terms, of the conflict between her obligation to her father and her own need for order in her state. Earlier, when she addressed her father directly, her statements of this conflict were extremely oblique (see TLN 712-25, 746-61; 1.4.201-14, 237-52). The passage below, found only in the Folio, provides her with a chance to expound the same idea with a simplicity that neither her husband nor anyone in the audience might misconstrue:

> *Gon.* This man hath had good Counsell,
> A hundred Knights?
> 'Tis politike, and safe to let him keepe
> At point a hundred Knights: yes, that on everie dreame,
> Each buz, each fancie, each complaint, dislike,
> He may enguard his dotage with their powres,
> And hold our lives in mercy. Oswald, I say.
> *Alb.* Well, you may feare too farre.
> *Gon.* Safer then trust too farre;
>   [Folio, 842-50; 1.4.322-28]

In his speech, Albany does not object that Goneril may irretrievably break the bond upon which Lear ceded his power. Goneril, in Albany's view, is not wrong but simply too extreme.

Thus, in the opening movements of the play, we find speeches added to Albany's part in the Folio, lines added in the Folio to the parts of characters addressing Albany, and details in the Folio added to speeches referring to Albany. These additions create for the audience an image of a man who might be sympathetic to Lear in other circumstances, but who is caught up by and succumbs to the stresses of conflicting loyalties and conflicting values.

The beginning of this play shows the audience the incredibly moral figures of Cordelia and Kent in actions of principled resistance that are practically suicidal. In contrast, Albany departs, not to be seen again for 1500 lines, offering only a murmured dissent:

> *Gon.* ... Your [*sic*] are much more at task for want of wisedome,
> Then prai'sd for harmefull mildnesse.
> *Alb.* How farre your eies may pierce I cannot tell;
> Striving to better, oft we marre what's well.
> *Gon.* Nay then——
> *Alb.* Well, well, the'vent.   *Exeunt*
> [Folio, 867-72; 1.4.343-47]

Morality and action should go hand in hand. Sir Philip Sidney said, "Not Gnosis but Praxis must be the fruit."[3] In this drama of sharply defined morality, Albany possesses a unique moral ambiguity, visible already in the first act of the play. The variants found in the Folio compound this ambiguity. He perceives rightly, but he takes no action.

Although Albany remains offstage until the second scene of the fourth act, in the interim several significant variants add more details to the audience's perception of his character and the themes related to his actions. In 1.4, lines unique to the Folio clarified Goneril's conflict between duty and domestic "tranquility"; similarly, speeches only in the Folio version of 2.4 give Regan a simple restatement of her thoughts on filial obligation and regal control. The two speeches in boldface below appear only in the Folio:

> *Reg.* I pray you Sir, take patience, I have hope
> You lesse know how to value her desert,
> Then she to scant her dutie.
> **Lear. Say? How is that?**
> **Reg. I cannot thinke my Sister in the least**
> **Would faile her Obligation. If Sir perchance**
> **She have restrained the Riots of your Followres,**
> **'Tis on such ground, and to such wholesome end,**
> **As cleeres her from all blame.**
> *Lear.* My curses on her.
> [Folio, 1416-25; 2.4.138-46]

Order and obligation are here again juxtaposed in a variant passage.

The important Folio variant in Kent's long speech to the Gentleman in 3.1 gives the audience a distinctly negative report about Albany. The Quarto text provides only another statement of the rumored hostility between Albany and Cornwall. The Folio, however, specifically links Albany with Cornwall in the offenses against Lear:

> *Kent.* . . . What hath bin seene,
> Either in snuffes, and packings of the Dukes,
> Or the hard Reine which both of them hath borne
> Against the old kinde King;
> [Folio, 1634-37; 3.1.25-28]

The opposition drawn again in the Folio version of Kent's speech is that between "the hard Reine" and "the old *kinde* King." The unimpeded will of the heads of state is set against their familial obligations to the man who entitled them to power, the prerogatives of authority versus the reponsibilities of authority. Albany, at this stage of the play, is described to the audience as practically identical to Cornwall in his failure to fulfill his obligation to Lear.

The audience's essentially negative perception of Albany is reinforced in 3.7 by Cornwall's confident faith in the cooperation of his brother-in-law when he sends Goneril and Edmund to Albany with news of the French Army:

> *Corn.* Poste speedily to my Lord your husband, shew him this Letter, the Army of France is landed: . . .
> . . . Advice the Duke where you are going, to a most festinate preparation: we are bound to the like. Our Postes shall be swift, and intelligent betwixt us.
> [Folio, 2060-61, 2068-70; 3.7.1-2, 9-12]

Despite the repeated rumors of division between the dukes, the audience is led to believe that they agree in their "Reine" against Lear and in their opposition to forces coming to aid him.

Not until the beginning of 4.2 is Albany presented as anything other than one of the group of Lear's oppressors. The audience, like Goneril, Edmund, and Oswald, must be surprised by Albany's reported withdrawal from his earlier acquiescence to his wife and her policies. The opening lines of the scene in which Albany makes his radical change stress the unexpectedness of the duke's actions:

> *Enter Gonerill, Bastard, and Steward.*
> *Gon.* Welcome my Lord. I mervell our mild husband
> Not met us on the way. Now, where's your Master?
> *Stew.* Madam within, but never man so chang'd:
> I told him of the Army that was Landed:
> He smil'd at it. I told him you were comming,
> His answer was, the worse. Of Glosters Treachery,
> And of the loyall Service of his Sonne
> When I inform'd him, then he call'd me Sot,
> And told me I had turn'd the wrong side out:
> What most he should dislike, seemes pleasant to him;
> What like, offensive.
> [Folio, 2267-78; 4.2.1-11]

Although this passage is identical in the two early texts, it should strike more surprisingly in the Folio because the Folio's additional material associates Albany more completely with the ideals and interests of Goneril's party.

The major variants in 4.2 illustrate how Albany's part

changes in the latter portion of *King Lear*. The earlier variants have all been accomplished by the addition of words, lines, and speeches. For Albany's part, the predominant mode of variation in 4.2 and succeeding scenes is cutting. (The second type of variant, important in the last scene, 5.3, is the transfer of speeches from one character to another.)

The earlier additions served to identify Albany as one who gave his tacit permission for Goneril's abrogation of the bonds of familial duty and gratitude. The cuts in 4.2 seem to serve a related purpose: the lines omitted from the Folio are precisely those stressing Albany's conscious articulation of and personal adherence to the value of respect for parents and benefactors. The lines remaining in his role are those expressing his new hostility to his wife, but they yield no hint of his own beliefs. The passages following come from the Quarto text; those not in the Folio are in boldface.

> *Gon.* I have beene worth the whistling.
> *Alb.* O Gonoril, you are not worth the dust which the rude wind
> Blowes in your face, **I feare your disposition**
> **That nature which contemnes ith origin**
> **Cannot be bordered certaine in it selfe,**
> **She that her selfe will sliver and disbranch**
> **From her materiall sap, perforce must wither,**
> **And come to deadly use.**
> [Quarto, H3^v; 4.2.29-37]

The references to "origin," "sap," and "branch" assert Albany's association with a positive, natural value system. They are not in the Folio.

> ***Gon.* No more, the text is foolish.**
> ***Alb.* Wisedome and goodnes, to the vild seeme vild,**
> **Filths savor but themselves, what have you done?**
> **Tigers, not daughters, what have you perform'd?**
> **A father, and a gracious aged man**
> **Whose reverence even the head-lugd beare would lick.**
> **Most barbarous, most degenerate have you madded,**
> **Could my good brother suffer you to doe it?**

> A man, a Prince, by him so benifited,
> If that the heavens doe not their visible spirits
> Send quickly downe to tame this vild offences, it will come
> Humanity must perforce pray on itself like monsters of the deepe.
>
> [Quarto, H3ᵛ-H4; 4.2.37-50]

In the Folio Goneril's line associating Albany's speech with a preacher's Biblical topic for a sermon is eliminated. Then Albany's references to wisdom, goodness, grace, reverence, and the obligation of gratitude are removed.

> *Gon.* Milke liverd man
> That bearest a cheeke for bloes, a head for wrongs,
> Who hast not in thy browes an eye deserning thine honour,
> From thy suffering, **that not know'st, fools do those vilains pitty**
> **Who are punisht ere they have done their mischiefe,**
> **Wher's thy drum? France spreds his banners in our noyseles land,**
> **With plumed helme, thy state begins thereat**
> **Whil'st thou a morall foole sits still and cries**
> **Alack why does he so?**
>   *Alb.* See thy selfe devill, proper deformity shewes not in the fiend, so horrid as in woman.
>   *Gon.* O vaine foole!
>
> [Quarto, H4; 4.2.50-61]

Goneril's shrill counsel of Machiavellian virtues and *forte main* would certainly help the audience to locate Albany somewhere near an opposite pole in a defined universe of values. Her speech, however, is truncated in the Folio as Albany vigorously interrupts her. Finally, the Folio lacks Albany's expression of his own forbearance from violent assault because of his moral compunctions about striking a female:

> *Alb.* **Thou changed, and selfe-coverd thing for shame**
> **Be-monster not thy feature, wer't my fitnes**
> **To let these hands obay my bloud,**
> **They are apt enough to dislecate and teare**

> **Thy flesh and bones, how ere thou art a fiend,**
> **A womans shape doth shield thee.**
> ***Gon.* Marry your manhood mew- - -**
> [Quarto, H4, corrected; 4.2.61-67]

What remains in Albany's role after these expressions of his values are cut from the Folio? Only two speeches declare Albany's moral system, fiercely and unequivocally:

> *Alb.* This shewes you are above
> You Justices, that these our neather crimes
> So speedily can venge. But (O poore Glouster)
> Lost he his other eye?
>
> *Alb.* Glouster, I live
> To thanke thee for the love thou shew'dst the King,
> And to revenge thine eyes. Come hither Friend,
> Tell me what more thou know'st.
> [Folio, 2323-26, 2344-47; 4.2.78-81, 94-97]

The common theme of these two speeches is vengeance. In the Folio version of this scene, these are the only statements by Albany that have any specifically moral content. Albany interprets Cornwall's death as a form of heavenly justice, enacted through the agency of Cornwall's servant. Further, he vows that he himself will become an agent of revenge. He assumes, of course, that he is on the side of the heavenly justice.

This passage is a radical departure by Shakespeare from a corresponding incident in his source, *The True Chronicle Historie of King Leir*. In that play, Cambria, the character equivalent to Shakespeare's Albany, specifically *rejects* the impulse expressed by his wife to take vengeance into her own hands:

> *Ragan.* . . . O, I do feare some charme or invocation
> Of wicked spirits, or infernall fiends,
> Stirred by Cordella, moves this innovation,
> And brings my father timeless to his end.
> But might I know, that the detested Witch
> Were certayne cause of this uncertayne ill,
> My selfe to Fraunce would go in some disguise,

    And with these nayles scratch out her hatefull eyes:
    For since I am deprived of my father,
    I loath my life, and wish my death the rather.
      Cambria. The heavens are just, and hate impiety,
    And will (no doubt) reveal such haynous crimes:
    Censure not any, till you know the right:
    Let him be Judge, that bringeth truth to light.[4]

In the remainder of the scene in the source play, Cambria repeatedly advocates temperance and the suspension of judgment until all evidence may be gathered and sifted. In contrast, Shakespeare's Albany proceeds in the opposite order; in his two moralizing speeches (quoted above) Albany first gives judgment and only then asks for more facts. In the Quarto, Albany achieves the same moral elevation observed in Cambria in the source play. In the Folio, however, he gives no evidence of any high moral discrimination.

Once again, the importance of these passages in the Folio is critically different even though the remaining words are identical to those in the Quarto. The longer Quarto version places Albany's few remarks on vengeance in a context of moral expressions identifying him with those values espoused by the party of Lear, Cordelia, Kent, Gloucester, and Edgar. In such a context, Albany is not seen by the audience as a person with only a single moral note. In the Folio, however, the audience hears nothing else. The surprising change in the Quarto is that Albany in 4.2 abruptly emerges as a character with a complete moral system, sharply opposed to that of his wife. In the Folio, however, Albany is sharply opposed to his wife, but his moral position remains relatively nebulous. Divine revenge as a principle of belief still allows a wide range of possible moral postures on other issues central to *King Lear*.

I do not mean that Albany is not suddenly perceived as a sympathetic character by the audience. Indeed, in several productions I attended, when Albany said "Oh Gonerill, / You are not worth the dust which the rude winde / Blowes in your face," the audience broke into cheers and applause. That response seems built into the line and the dramatic situation. It must be stressed, nevertheless, that Albany in the

Folio seems to espouse no positively defined ethical standards. Precisely this ambiguity in his character continues to be the subject of and apparent intention behind the important differences between the Folio and the Quarto versions of later scenes in *King Lear*.

The audience observes that at the end of 4.2 a schism exists between Albany and his wife. They exit separately, Goneril with her letter from Regan, and Albany with the messenger who sympathetically reported Gloucester's blinding and the deaths of Cornwall and his servant. The stage action implies a new alignment of power may result from Albany's change of heart.

In the scenes immediately following 4.2, the Quarto and the Folio gave very different sequences of narrative details related to Albany's behavior in the final act of the play. Lines unique to the Quarto build up a series of references and actions that will, in the Quarto version of 5.1, allow Albany to justify his decision when he goes to fight against Cordelia's army. Variants in the Folio version systematically remove Albany's "patriotic" justification.

Perhaps most important, the two texts present the opposing armies in different lights. In the Quarto, the force coming to aid Lear is repeatedly identified as the army of France. Kent tells of it first in the Quarto version of 3.1. Gloucester speaks of this army as "part of a power already landed" in the Quarto version of 3.3. Both texts have Cornwall report "The army of France is landed"—the only point in the Folio where Lear's friends are identified as a French power. In only the Quarto text of 4.2 does Goneril say "France spreads his banners in our noyseles land." In 4.3, a scene unique to the Quarto, Kent and a Gentleman talk about the army of the King of France, now under the command of "The Marshall of France Monsier la Far."

In an oddly disjointed dialogue in 4.3, the Quarto also reports that Albany is one of the leaders of the British force:

> *Kent.* Of Albanies and Cornewals powers you heard not.
> *Gent.* Tis so they are a foote.
>
> [Quarto, I1; 4.3.48-49]

Two problems here are, first, that we learned in the scene before of Cornwall's death and, second, that in the last speech of the previous scene Albany vowed to avenge Gloucester's blinding. Only fifty lines later we hear that Albany leads a force allied with Gloucester's tormentors. In the Quarto the details we get seem precise, but they raise genuine confusions.

A quite different narrative order exists in the Folio. Just as this version withholds the news of the French landing until five hundred lines after it is reported in the Quarto, the Folio also delays indicating a name for the leader of the British force, and the Folio gives only a strong suggestion of who leads the French. After Goneril and Albany depart in apparent hostility at the end of 4.2, the Folio text has Cordelia enter at the head of her forces: *"Enter with Drum and Colours, Cordelia, Gentlemen, and Souldiours."* In the absence of any references to the French king or to a French general, duke, or even knight, the audience naturally perceives Cordelia herself as the commander of the army. She receives the news of the approaching British. She also issues the command to send soldiers out in search of Lear. Whether indeed she is the leader is immaterial. According to the Folio text only Cordelia acts like the leader.

The audience is given the heartening display of two attractive figures, first Albany and then Cordelia thirty lines later, profoundly dedicating themselves to the rescue and restoration of Lear and his friends:

Alb. Glouster, I live
To thanke thee for the love thou shew'dst the King,
And to revenge thine eyes.
      [Folio, 2344-46; 4.2.94-96]

Cor. . . . O deere Father,
It is thy businesse that I go about: Therfore great France
My mourning, and importun'd teares hath pittied:
No blowne Ambition doth our Armes incite,
But love, deere love, and our ag'd Fathers Rite:
      [Folio, 2376-80; 4.4.23-28]

In the Quarto and in the modern composite texts, because they contain 4.3, there is a painful irony in this juxtaposition of similar intent by the leaders of two armies about to fight against one another. No such irony exists in the Folio text, because the clues needed to discover Albany's position relative to his wife, his sister-in-law Regan, and his sister-in-law Cordelia have been carefully obscured, erased, or altered. When Cordelia's messenger in 4.4 reports the approach of the British, an audience watching a production that follows the Folio text does not necessarily associate this army with the Duke of Albany.

In the Folio, without any prior identification of Albany as the leader of the British, the dialogue between Regan and Oswald at the beginning of 4.5 becomes a far more disturbing and problematic exchange for the audience.

> *Enter Regan, and Steward.*
> *Reg.* But are my Brothers Powres set forth?
> *Stew.* I madam,
> *Reg.* Himselfe in person there?
> *Stew.* Madam with much ado:
> Your Sister is the better Souldier.
> [Folio, 2383-88; 4.5.1-4]

Because 4.3 is in the Quarto and in the composite text, this interchange reports little new information other than that Albany is not a very good military man. The same lines in the Folio, however, indicate for the first time in that text that Albany may enter the conflict allied with his wife and Regan rather than with Cordelia. Unlike the unequivocal message given in the Quarto that Albany was part of the British force, in their Folio context the lines quoted above present Albany as if he may have ambiguous loyalties. Regan's second question, "Himselfe in person there?" seems to be her attempt to ascertain exactly where Albany stands. Oswald's flippant reply does little to settle the matter.

During the following scene, 4.6, the action occurs in the fields near Dover where the opposing armies are approaching. Two references to Albany, by Lear and by Edgar, again give the audience confusing messages about his character. Lear, in his moments of gnomic lucidity, rails against the administrators of law. He sees himself as a protector of those, like Gloucester, whom authority abuses. In one of the great emotional climaxes of the play, the king imagines an attack on the two heads of state now responsible for corrupted justice:

> It were a delicate stratagem, to shoo
> A Troope of Horse with Felt: Ile put't in proofe,
> And when I have stolne upon these Son in Lawes,
> Then kill, kill, kill, kill, kill, kill.
> [Folio, 2626-29; 4.6.184-87]

In his wild outcry Lear would kill "these Son in Lawes," both of them. At least for the moment, Albany stands in Lear's mind as one of his enemies.

Only one hundred lines later, however, Edgar discovers Goneril's letters, learns that Albany may also be Goneril's victim, and reintroduces the possibility that Albany yet may be extricated from his bondage. The hope for Lear's rescue offered to the audience at the end of Albany's scene with his wife (4.2) and through all of Cordelia's appearance with her army (4.4) may still come to pass:

> Oh indi[sti]nguish'd space of Womans will,
> A plot upon her vertuous Husbands life,
> And the exchange my Brother: heere, in the sands
> Thee Ile rake up, the poste unsanctified
> Of murtherous Letchers: and in the mature time,
> With this ungracious paper strike the sight
> Of the death-practis'd Duke: for him 'tis well,
> That of thy death, and businesse, I can tell.
> [Folio, 2724-31; 4.6.271-78]

This is only the first time in the play that another character assumes that Albany is "vertuous," except, of course, for Lear in the first scene. Edgar's characterization of Albany must still be seen within the context of all the other conflicting signals about him. It should not be taken as the correct or authoritative judgment.

Albany's position in the conflict between Lear and Cordelia on the one hand and Goneril, Regan, and Edmund on the other is the subject of the action in his next scene, 5.1. In the Quarto and the modern composite text Albany's actions and his justifications quickly become clear. In the Folio his actions are clear, but the reasons for them remain nebulous. As the scene opens, both Edmund and Regan question whether Albany is committed to fight with them in the forthcoming battle:

> *Bast.* Know of the Duke if his last purpose hold,
> Or whether since he is advis'd by ought
> To change the course, he's full of alteration,
> And selfereproving, bring his constant pleasure.
> *Reg.* Our Sisters man is certainely miscarried.
> *Bast.* 'Tis to be doubted Madam.
> [Folio, 2847-52; 5.1.1-6]

However, when Albany enters fifteen lines later in the scene, the Quarto version of the passage eliminates any doubts about his course of action or the motives behind it:

> *Enter Albany and Gonorill with troupes.*
> *Gono.* I had rather loose the battaile, then that sister should loosen him and mee.
> *Alb.* Our very loving sister well be-met
> For this I heare the King is come to his daughter
> With others, whome the rigour of our state
> Forst to crie out, where I could not be honest
> I never yet was valiant, for this busines
> It touches us, as France invades our land
> Not bolds the King, with others whome I feare,
> Most just and heavy causes make oppose.
> *Bast.* Sir you speake nobly. *Reg.* Why is this reason'd?
> *Gono.* Combine togither gainst the enemy,
> For these domestique dore particulars
> Are not to question here.
> *Alb.* Let us then determine with the auntient of warre
> on our proceedings. *Bast.* I shall attend you presently
> at your tent.
> [Quarto, K3; 5.1.18-33]

Albany's thinking about his part in the ensuing battle springs forth as a fully worked out choice between conflicting values —defense of the realm outweighs obligation to Lear and "just" rebels. Albany announces the results of his considerations. He justifies his action solely on the grounds that Cordelia's army is French.

The speeches of his three comrades-in-arms, in the context of the Quarto, simply acknowledge and affirm the "virtue" of Albany's decision. Goneril effectively summarizes Albany's argument, eliminating the compunctions about fighting Lear and the rebellious British by labelling them "domestique dore particulars," insignificant before the main assault of "the enemy" from France. Albany's last speech in this exchange signifies he is satisfied that his allies understand and accept the specific terms under which he is engaged with them.

Cuts in the Folio text in this same passage create an entirely different dramatic action for Albany's speech, change the meanings and functions of the replies of Goneril and Regan, and alter Edmund's participation in the exchange. The seven speeches covering sixteen lines in the Quarto text are reduced to four speeches and ten lines in the Folio.

> *Enter with Drum and Colours, Albany, Gonerill, Soldiers.*
> *Alb.* Our very loving Sister, well be-met:
> Sir, this I heard, the King is come to his Daughter
> With others, whom the rigour of our State
> Forc'd to cry out.
> *Regan.* Why is this reasond?
> *Gone.* Combine together 'gainst the Enemie:
> For these domesticke and particurlar broiles,
> Are not the question heere.
> *Alb.* Let's then determine with th'ancient of warre
> On our proceeding.
> [Folio, 2864-74; 5.1.20-32]

First, the elimination of Goneril's speech at the entrance concentrates the attention of the audience immediately upon Albany. The subject of the passage, first raised at the beginning of the scene, will be Albany's decision. The issue of romantic intrigue, which occupies Edmund and Regan before Albany's entrance, is suspended in the Folio rather than extended into the new dramatic sequence as it is in the Quarto.

Second, Albany's speech now in no way justifies his participation in the war. Instead he raises a strong objection to fighting against the opposing army. Albany's announcement about Lear, Cordelia, and rebel Englishmen implies that because he has come into the field only to fight an army of Frenchmen he must reconsider his participation. The Folio's version of Albany's speech implies that he sees a real conflict in his loyalties; perhaps his "very loving Sister," his estranged wife, and Gloucester's unkind bastard may not be the best choice of allies.

Third, although Edmund's two speeches are removed from the Folio, he rather than Regan is addressed by Albany. Edmund is asked to participate in the consideration of Albany's news, whereas in the Quarto he was simply an interlocutor with little active involvement. Edmund's first speech in this passage, "Sir you speake nobly," would serve no purpose in the Folio version of Albany's speech. The duke has not delivered a "noble" rationalization for a questionable moral decision. He has only questioned the decision.

Fourth, in its new context in the Folio, Regan's question "Why is this reasond?" takes on a new meaning. She asks Albany "Why are you raising this embarrassing new issue?" instead of "Why are you troubling us with your moralizing over an obviously correct decision?" In its Quarto context, Regan perceives Albany's full speech as a simple pause in the action while the principals greet one another. But when, in the Folio, Albany announces only his doubts without his justifications, she perceives his speech as a threat to their entire enterprise.

Fifth, in its Folio context, it is Goneril's brisk speech ("Combine together 'gainst the Enemie . . ."), rather than his own rationalization, that convinces Albany to enter the battle. Under the pressure of her personality, Albany lays aside his scruples about the presence of disaffected relatives and wayward friends within the camp of "the Enemie." She, rather than he, initially offers the argument that the larger issue of the safety of England must be placed above considerations of allegiance to family and friend.

Sixth, Albany's speech, "Let's then determine . . . ," means, in the Folio, "I will withdraw my objection." As in many other places in the Folio, Albany's action here is left without any articulated explanation. The audience sees only that Albany acquiesces to Goneril's course of action despite his own misgivings. The events here resemble those seen earlier when Albany first objected to Goneril's treatment of Lear but then failed to curb her offenses (1.4). In its Folio context only, this instant of decision presents to the audience an example of what Maynard Mack describes as one of the distinguishing characteristics of the dramaturgy of *King Lear*: "Instead of scenes according to the genesis or gestation of action, . . . *King Lear* offers us the moment at which will converts into its outward expressions of action and consequence, and this fact, I suspect, helps account for the special kind of painfulness that the play always communicates to its audiences."[5] The elaborate excuse that Albany is morally bound to defend England against the "foreign invader" vanishes from the Folio. In fact, with the exception of Cornwall's announcement in 3.7, "The Army of France is landed," every reference to Cordelia's army as being French has been cut from the Folio. Albany's justification is replaced by the bare event of his decision.

In summary, the Quarto version of this passage yields a more comprehensible, straightforward reading for Albany's character. But the Folio provides better drama. The Quarto gives the audience the reason for Albany's choice; the Folio offers the audience only the painful moment of choice itself.

Immediately following the action analyzed above, while Edmund, Goneril and Regan exit, Edgar interrupts Albany's exit to hand him the letter Goneril wrote to Edmund suggesting murder. Again, although the passage is nearly identical in the Quarto and the Folio, the altered context in the Folio creates new meanings and new dramatic actions. The basis for the difference in the Folio is that Albany in that text has not decided to fight against Cordelia for any profound reason; instead he was influenced by Goneril's forceful presence. But the incriminating letter, which has been displayed and read aloud and spoken of onstage over and over again, will once again remind Albany of the truth about his allies. Thus, after Goneril leaves the stage, the strong possibility arises that

Albany may be influenced by the testimony of the letter to change his decision.

Despite any affirmation of the evil natures of his friends, both in the Quarto and in the composite texts Albany is honor-bound to fight the battle because the enemy is French. He has already overcome the difficulty that his opponents include Lear, Cordelia, and many good Englishmen. Further evidence of his own comrades' perfidy would not deter him from using them as questionable means to achieve what he has concluded is a justifiable end, repelling the French invader. But in the Folio, Albany does not have his own reasoned, moral justification for fighting, merely Goneril's assertion that his doubts "are not the question here." The letter delivered by Edgar could serve as a stimulus to make Albany again reject his wife for her outrageous acts, just as he did earlier in their confrontation in 4.2. In the Folio, Albany's quiescent moral sensibility may awaken *if* he reads the letter.

Simple variants just after Edgar exits underscore the dramatic tension concentrated upon Albany's possession of Goneril's letter in the Folio. According to the Quarto, Edmund rushes in with a purely verbal report of the threatening approach of the opposing army. Edmund's urgent concern about the enemy's unfathomed "great strength" commands Albany's attention more forcefully than the letter in his hand:

> *Alb.* Stay till I have read the letter.
> *Edg.* I was forbid it, when time shall serve let but the Herald cry and ile appeare againe.   *Exit.*
> *Alb.* Why fare thee well, I will ore-looke the paper.
>   *Enter Edmund.*
> *Bast.* The enemies in vew, draw up your powers
> Hard is the quesse of their great strength and forces
> By diligent discovery, but your hast is now urg'd on you.
> *Alb.* Wee will greet the time.   *Exit.*
>   [Quarto, K3^v; 5.1.47-54]

In contrast, the corresponding passage in the Folio shows Edmund with a written, rather than an oral, report of the enemy's "true strength," as opposed to its "great strength." And, I believe, Edmund hands this paper to Albany:

> *Bast.* The Enemy's in view, draw up your powers,
> **Heere** is the guesse of their **true** strength and Forces,
> By dilligent discoverie, but your hast
> Is now urg'd on you.
>   [Folio, 2897-2900; 5.1.51-54;
>   boldface indicates Folio alterations.]

In this version, Albany holds two letters. The one handed him by Edgar perhaps may lead him to forego or postpone the battle. The one from Edmund will aid him in pursuing the engagement. Albany stands for an instant with important missives given to him from two sides. He resembles at this moment Julius Caesar on his way to the Capitol, given one letter from Artemidorus which, if read, may prompt him to a safe course, and a second letter from Decius, which will lead him to disaster (*Julius Caesar*, 3.1; TLN 1206-15). Indeed, the image of a character suspended between alternatives is repeated immediately after Albany's exit as Edmund addresses the audience:

> To both these Sisters have I sworne my love:
> Each jealous of the other, as the stung
> Are of the Adder. Which of them shall I take?
> Both? One? Or neither?
>   [Folio, 2902-5; 5.1.55-58]

Albany's options are superficially the same in both texts: immediately to follow the martial course urged by Edmund or momentarily to pause for consideration of Edgar's humble appeal. Only in the Folio, however, do the letters he holds have the power to swing him into or away from the ensuing battle. At the crucial moment he turns and rushes out to "greet the time." He'll fight.

The systematic difference between the versions is the presentation of Albany carefully weighing his choices with clearly defined and articulated moral certainty in the Quarto and in modern composite texts and his appearance in the Folio, where he repeatedly makes hasty and ill-considered decisions in a state of moral ambiguity strongly influenced by Goneril, Regan, and Edmund.

In a theatrical presentation following the Folio text, I believe the events of this scene ought to rush in upon Albany. He should have no time to read the first letter from Edgar before Edmund intercedes with the second. The Folio seems to call for an acceleration of the pace. In contrast, most modern productions following the Quarto or its close derivative, the composite text, slow the pace here. Albany takes time to read Edgar's letter, gradually understands its significance, stares coldly at Edmund during his call to urgent action, and then haughtily stalks offstage, proud of his own forbearance and confident of his moral superiority.[6] Both versions work. But Albany performs different actions according to the text one follows.

Act 5, Scene 3

Albany reaches his fullest dramatic development in the final scene of the play, 5.3. Thirty of Albany's speeches, more than half the total in his part, are in this scene. Lear himself is onstage for roughly one-third of the scene, Albany for slightly more than two-thirds. The scene contains approximately seventeen major variants, far more than any other scene in the play. Sixteen of these are directly related to Albany's role; only one affects Lear.

The variants here that are considered significant for the purpose of this study create new patterns of stage events in the Folio. Included are additions of new speeches, cuts of entire speeches or of major portions, reattributions of speeches from one character to another, complete reworkings of dialogue passages, and obvious changes in entrances and exits. Omitted from this discussion are the addition or cutting of individual words or phrases, as well as the substitution of equivalent words. These would bring the total number of variants to approximately two hundred, again the largest number for any scene in the play.

Albany's role in this final scene may be broken into three important dramatic segments. The first runs from his entrance until the moment Edmund falls, concluding the trial by combat. In this section the Folio version, far more than the

Quarto, creates the impression that Albany commands every aspect of the action. The second section of the scene extends from the immediate aftermath of the trial until the entrance of Lear. Textual variants in this part of the scene repeatedly alter Albany's behavior during his moments of great emotional stress. In addition, variants in the Folio focus attention upon Albany's reactions to the major events in this central section. The third part of the scene, from Lear's entrance until the end of the play, includes Albany's response to the sight of Lear and Cordelia and his two abdication speeches. The only significant variant related to Albany in this final section transfers the last speech in the play from Albany to Edgar. Almost all the variants earlier in this scene appear to point toward this final moment. This scene resolves the issue of Albany's suitability as a ruler at the end of the play, and it provides important clues for understanding Albany's two acts of abdication.

The first changes in the Folio version of this climactic scene that affect Albany's development are found at his entry with Goneril and Regan. The immediate context and the spectacular display for his entrance are both different in the Folio text. Just before the entrance, the second speech for Edmund's Captain (explaining why he will agree to "great employment,") is not in the Folio: "I cannot draw a cart, nor eate dride oats, / If it bee mans worke ile do't." The Captain's line resembles Albany's self-justification in 5.1, which was also removed from the Folio. In the Quarto text, both Albany in 5.1 and the Captain here attempt to rationalize their obviously questionable moral choices. The Folio versions of both passages in contrast show only the decisions being made, not the reasoning behind them. Thus Albany returns to the stage only a moment after the audience observes another immoral but "practical" and "timely" assault initiated against Lear and Cordelia. Indeed, Edmund's sententious lines to his Captain recall Goneril's lecture to Albany in the earlier scene, when she advised him to think that "these domesticke and particurlar broiles, / Are not the question heere":

Bast. . . . know thou this, that men
Are as the time is; to be tender minded

Do's not become a Sword, thy great imployment
Will not beare question:
> [Folio, 2973-76; 5.3.30-33]

Both Albany in 5.1 and the Captain immediately before Albany's entrance in 5.3 evidently act upon the conviction that for a special time one's normal morality may or must be suspended: "men / Are as the time is."

Into this dramatic context, Albany, Goneril, and Regan enter to the accompaniment of a trumpet "flourish," called for only in the Folio's stage direction. Distinguishable from the "sennet" that sounds as Lear enters in the opening scene of the play and the "tucket" that announces Goneril's arrival at Gloucester's castle in 2.4, this particular call is added at other moments in the Folio to mark peculiarly inauspicious ceremonies. The entrance of France and Burgundy after Cordelia has lost her dowry is heralded by a flourish, as is Lear's abrupt exit with the Duke of Burgundy near the end of the same scene. This spectacular ornament in the Folio's stage direction here heightens the contrast between Lear and Cordelia, who have just left the stage bound and under guard, and Albany's party coming onstage in celebration of their triumph.

In the unfolding of this scene, it is very important to notice what the characters actually say—and do *not* say. For example, in Albany's entrance speech, he demands that Edmund deliver Lear and Cordelia to him. This part of his speech raises the possibility that Lear and Cordelia may be rescued. Edmund's Captain has departed just seconds before. He may easily be called back. In his speech Albany does not propose to return Lear and Cordelia immediately to any loving reunion, however. Earlier, in 5.1, Edmund introduced *his* idea of what Albany would do after the battle:

> ... As for the mercie
> Which he intends to Lear and to Cordelia,
> The Battaile done, and they within our power,
> Shall never see his pardon: for my state,
> Stands on me to defend, not to debate.
> [Folio, 2912-16; 5.1.65-69]

But when Albany himself finally articulates the moral principles which will govern his treatment of Lear and Cordelia the audience hears no word of mercy. Instead, he intends to balance two conflicting appeals:

> I do require them of you so to use them,
> As we shall find *their merites, and our safety*
> May *equally* determine.
> [Folio, 2986-88; 5.3.43-45;
> my italics added for emphasis]

Albany certainly does not espouse the Machiavellian principles shared by Goneril and Edmund, but clearly he does not intend, like Cordelia, to "forget, and forgive." He simply does not use such words. He will judge: "their merites, and our safety."

The next action in the scene, Edmund's attempt to deny the prisoners to Albany, takes different forms in the Quarto and the Folio. Albany's response to Edmund, though the same in both versions, acquires different meanings in the variant contexts. In the following passage, the lines in boldface do not appear in the Folio:

> *Bast.* Sir I thought it fit,
> To send the old and miserable King to some retention,
>   and appointed guard,
> Whose age has charmes in it, whose title more,
> To pluck the common bossome of his side,
> And turne our imprest launces in our eyes
> Which doe commaund them, with him I sent the queen
> My reason, all the same and they are readie to morrow,
> Or at further space, to appeare where you shall hold
> Your session **at this time, wee sweat and bleed,**
> **The friend hath lost his friend and the best quarrels**
> **In the heat are curst, by those that feele their sharpnes,**
> **The question of Cordelia and her father**
> **Requires a fitter place.**
>   *Alb.* Sir by your patience,
> I hold you but a subject of this warre, not as a brother.
> [Quarto, K4^v; 5.3.45-61]

Here, in the longer Quarto version, the speech has two main parts. First Edmund explains why he has sent Lear and Cordelia away, and then he gives a reason for not judging their case at the present moment. In the Quarto this second part of the speech, Edmund's sententious counsel—suggesting that Albany may not be a cool or impartial judge of their recent foes, Lear and Cordelia—prompts Albany's reminder to Edmund that he should know and keep his place.

Without the last five lines of Edmund's speech, the Folio calls attention to the earlier part of the speech as the only possible source of Albany's irritation with Edmund. In their substance, the first nine lines of Edmund's speech do little else than vividly particularize Albany's vague references to "our safety" and to "the opposites of this dayes strife." Edmund's main point in the Folio is not Albany's temporary inability to judge a case fairly, but instead it is that he and Albany share a common danger. He says Lear's "charmes" and "title" may "turne *our* imprest launces in *our* eyes" (emphasis added). In the Folio, Albany is rejecting Edmund's suggestion that they both share in the risk of rebellion. Edmund's assumption that the army was in any way his own prompts Albany's reaction in the Folio, not his withholding of the prisoners nor his questioning of Albany's impartiality. Authority is the sole issue of Albany's reply in the Folio, not justice, the question in the Quarto.

In the exchange that follows Edmund's speech, all consideration of Lear and Cordelia is absent. Only at his entrance does Albany demand custody of them to judge "their merites, and our safety." But thereafter, until the entrance of Kent nearly two hundred lines later, Albany considers little but his security as the head of the state. In his own words, Lear and Cordelia become for Albany a "great thing of us forgot."

The remainder of this section of the scene concerns Edmund's arraignment and trial by combat. In the Quarto version, four separate speeches stress that Edmund eagerly and aggressively suggests and helps conduct the test of his strength and "right." In contrast, six distinct variants in the Folio reduce Edmund's participation to that of simply accepting his role as the defendant in a case of treason; Albany is made to appear in total command of the proceedings.

The quarrel between Albany and Edmund first arises because Albany claims a right to determine whether Regan may invest Edmund with her power. In the Quarto version of the passage, Edmund rejects Albany's claim and appeals to the judgment of arms. In return, Albany abruptly changes the issue from Edmund's rights of marriage to a charge of "capitall treason," to be decided by combat.

> *Reg.* . . . Generall
> Take thou my souldiers, prisoners, patrimonie,
> Witnes the world that I create thee here
> My Lord and maister.
>   *Gon.* Meane you to injoy him then?
>   *Alb.* The let alone lies not in your good will.
>   *Bast.* Nor in thine Lord.
>   *Alb.* Halfe blouded fellow, yes.
>   *Bast.* Let the drum strike, and prove my title good.
>   *Alb.* Stay yet, heare reason, Edmund I arrest thee
> On capitall treason, . . .
> . . . .
> . . . thou art arm'd Gloster,
> If none appeare to prove upon thy head,
> Thy hainous, manifest, and many treasons,
> There is my pledge, ile prove it on thy heart
> Ere I tast bread, thou art in nothing lesse
> Then I have here proclaimd thee.
>   [Quarto, L1; 5.3.74-95]

Next, Edmund answers Albany's "pledge" by throwing his own "exhange," glove for glove or blow for blow, and he embellishes the ceremony by calling for trumpets to sound. Then when Albany calls for a herald, Edmund seconds him by exuberantly doubling the call:

>   *Bast.* Ther's my exchange, what in the world he is,
> That names me traytor, villain-like he lies,
> Call by thy trumpet, he that dares approach,
> On him, on you, who not, I will maintaine
> My truth and honour firmely.
>   *Alb.* A Herald ho.   *Bast.* A Herald ho, a Herald.
>   [Quarto, L1-L1ᵛ; 5.3.97-102]

And again, after the Herald formally announces the trial, Edmund gives the commands for the trumpets to sound:

> *Alb.* . . . Come hether Herald, let the trumpet sound,
> And read out this.   *Cap.* Sound trumpet?
> *Her.* If any man of qualitie or degree, in the hoast of the army, will maintaine upon Edmund supposed Earle of Gloster, that he's a manifold traitour, let him appeare at the third sound of the trumpet, he is bold in his defence.
> *Bast.* Sound?   Againe?
>   [Quarto, L1ᵛ; 5.3.108-17]

Vigorous and very theatrical, Edmund appears to be at the height of his audacious powers. Albany, forceful and steadfast against him, shows his own strength. But here the action is dominated by neither man.

A totally different sequence of events is found in the Folio. Edmund's challenge (which initiated the idea of an armed combat in the Quarto) is transferred to Regan and altered to fit her character. Regan says, "Let the Drum strike, and prove my title thine." She addresses Edmund, not Albany, and the speech reasonably serves as another step in Regan's ceremonial investment of dignity upon her beloved Edmund. From her lips, the speech is not a martial dare; Regan no longer possesses the feral strength she displayed when she slew Cornwall's servant. Goneril has poisoned her, and she is on the verge of physical collapse. Edmund's self-confident challenge in the Quarto becomes in the Folio Regan's proclamation of her love at the moment she feels her own impending death.

The second variant in this passage, an added interjection for Goneril ("An enterlude."), divides Albany's long speech into two sections: the first part contains Albany's formal charge against Edmund and his address to Regan; the latter part, containing another variant, in the Folio initiates the idea of a trial by combat.

> *Alb.* . . . If you will marry, make your loves to me,
> My Lady is bespoke.
> **Gon. An enterlude.**

> *Alb.* Thou art armed Gloster,
> **Let the Trmpet [sic] sound:**
> If none appeare . . .
>
>   . . . .
>   . . . Come hither Herald, let the Trumper [sic] sound,
> And read out this.   ***A Tumpet* [sic] *sounds*.**
>   ***Herald reads.***
> *If any man of qualitie or degree, within the lists of the Army, will maintaine upon Edmund, supposed Earle of Gloster, that he is a manifold Traitor, let him appeare by the third sound of the Trumpet: he is bold in his defence.*   ***1 Trumpet.***
>   *Her.* Againe.   ***2 Trumpet.***
>   *Her.* Againe.   ***3 Trumpet.***
>   [Folio, 3033-38, 3057-66; 5.3.88-91, 108-17;
>   boldface indicates material only in Folio]

Albany, not Edmund, proposes the trial first, and as a result of the Folio's third variant, he, rather than Edmund, first calls for the trumpet. It is Albany who eagerly presses for a confrontation. The fourth variant in this passage erases Edmund's repeated call for a herald. The fifth removes the Captain who in the Quarto relays Albany's call for trumpets; this leaves Albany asserting his control more personally. And finally, a sixth change in the Folio text has Albany's herald, rather than Edmund, give the last commands to the trumpeters.

The Folio version concentrates the audience's attention upon Albany as the commanding figure on the stage. The effect achieved here is similar to that of the Folio version of Albany's entrance at 5.1. Subsidiary voices are removed in order to let Albany stand out. Instead of presenting a balanced picture of Albany standing against Edmund, the dialogue in the Folio highlights Albany in the role of accuser and as the primary moving force. Simultaneously, the Folio reduces Edmund's participation. Again, either text gives strong, self-consistent actions.

There is no agreement among modern editors on how to choose between the Quarto and Folio versions of each of the six variants in this passage. For example, the five popular editions on my desk give four different patterns of dialogue and stage action, each editor basing his edition now on one text and now the other. But not one among them presents a script showing Edmund's aggressive involvement in the trial as in the Quarto, nor does any present a script showing Albany in absolute control as in the Folio. None of the modern composite editions makes as strong a dramatic statement as either of the two early texts. Choosing eclectically from two versions, modern editors produce relatively shapeless hybrids.

The second major section of this scene begins after Edmund falls mortally wounded at the end of his battle with Edgar. Six passages of dialogue, including all but four of Albany's fourteen speeches in this part of the scene, appear in distinct forms or in altered contexts in the Quarto and the Folio.

Immediately preceding and following Albany's display of Goneril's incriminating letter and her hasty exit, the dialogue governs an intricate series of stage movements: Albany gives the letter to either Goneril or Edmund to read, Albany prevents Goneril from tearing the paper, then she storms offstage, and Albany sends someone out to "governe" her. The two texts present interpretive problems about the precise direction of Albany's addresses and the timing of his actions. In the Quarto Albany works straightforwardly throughout the passage; in the Folio he delays momentarily before sending a guardian after Goneril.

Shakespeare's consistent handling of pronouns of address provides valuable clues for unravelling the action.[7] After Albany calls Edmund a "Halfe-blooded fellow" at TLN 3025, 5.3.81, he always addresses Edmund in familiar forms of personal pronouns, "thee" and "thou," ten times out of ten. Just as consistently, four times out of four, he uses the formal "you" and "your" when he speaks to Goneril and Regan. Following these cues, we see that Albany should turn from Goneril to Edmund in much the same way in both the Quarto and the Folio versions of his speech below. Bracketed insertions in italics are my own.

[*to Goneril:*] Stop your mouth dame, or with this paper shall I stople it, [*to Edmund:*] thou worse then any thing, reade thine owne evill, [*to Goneril:*] nay no tearing Lady, I perceive you know't.
                             [Quarto, L2; 5.3.155-58]

The Folio text marks the points of Albany's turns to Goneril and to Edmund with full colons. And a command, "hold Sir," even more clearly marks the address to Edmund:

Shut your mouth Dame,
Or with this paper shall I stop it: hold Sir,
Thou worse then any name, reade thine owne evill:
No tearing Lady, I perceive you know it.
                             [Folio, 3112-15; 5.3.155-58]

So Albany shows the letter to Goneril, hands it to Edmund to read, and then prevents Goneril from snatching it away for destruction. Many modern editions indicate that "thou worse then any name . . ." should be spoken to Goneril. But this demands that Albany address her with both formal and informal pronouns, within a single speech and with no noticeable motive for the alternation. This is improbable because of the careful distinctions found in Albany's earlier speeches.

Goneril's exit and Albany's response to it also have potentially confusing changes of address. Folio variants remove possible ambiguity. At the same time, however, the Folio variants introduce a change in Albany's character. In the following passage from the Quarto, it is not clear to whom Albany addresses his question, "know'st thou this paper?"

Alb. . . . Lady, I perceive you know't.
Gon. Say if I do, the lawes are mine not thine, who shal arraine me for't.
Alb. Most monstrous know'st thou this paper?
Gon. Aske me not what I know.   *Exit. Gonorill.*
Alb. Go after her, shee's desperate, governe her.
                             [Quarto, L2; 5.3.158-62]

At first glance it appears that Albany addresses Goneril in his first and second speeches here. On closer examination, however, it is noticed that Albany has just said to Goneril, concerning the letter, "I perceive you know't," so if he then should ask her in his very next speech if she knows the letter he would be acting very strangely. When pronouns of address are considered it seems more likely that Albany is addressing his question to Edmund, because he uses the familiar "thou." But Goneril, not Edmund, replies. It is conceivable that Albany does address Goneril, adopting the familiar form, but in this text the evidence is ambiguous.

The Folio version clarifies the details of this exchange. Goneril's exit is advanced to come after her previous speech, and her line, "Aske me not what I know," is transferred to Edmund's part.

> *Alb.* . . . Lady, I perceive you know it.
> *Gon.* Say if I do, the Lawes are mine not thine,
> Who can araigne me for't?   *Exit.*
> *Alb.* Most monstrous! O, know'st thou this paper?
> *Bast.* Aske me not what I know.
> *Alb.* Go after her, she's desperate, governe her.
>   [Folio, 3115-20; 5.3.158-62]

Goneril is gone, so Albany's question about the paper can only be directed to Edmund, in this text at least.

Albany in the Folio version, as a consequence of the variants, reacts to the events in a notably disjointed rhythm. He turns his attention from Goneril's exit back to Edmund to ask his question about the paper, next he hears Edmund's response, and only then does he send someone out to "governe" his wife. This kind of "irregularity" appears in Albany's role in this passage of the Folio and in Folio versions of two other exciting moments. Here and in the later instances Albany's pattern of delay seems to be a characteristic response to heightened emotional stress.

Delayed response in a case when we would expect an immediate reaction is a typical Shakespearean device for showing a character under great psychological pressure. An extreme example is found in *King John* (TLN 1902; 4.2.181), where John says, "My mother dead," fifty lines after he hears the news. Lear's reactions in 2.4 of this play also erupt at odd moments, clearly indicating his inner turmoil; for example, three lines after he calms himself, saying "Ile forbeare," he suddenly cries, "Death on my state: wherefore / Should he sit heere?" (TLN 1385-89; 2.4.109-13). The Folio shows Albany similarly out of synchronization.

Most modern editions follow the Quarto for Goneril's exit. Kenneth Muir's note in the New Arden edition seems to epitomize the approach of recent editors. (The New [Cambridge] editors, for example, quote Muir's analysis as their own justification for adopting the Quarto version over the Folio.) Muir argues: "[1] Goneril needs an hysterical, not a defiant, exit line; [2] Albany would not turn to Edmund to ask his question about the letter, and then belatedly give instructions about his wife; and [3] it is difficult to reconcile Edmund's confession ['What you have charged me with, that have I done . . .'] with his defiance two lines earlier" (p. 209). In reply to Muir's assertions, several questions must be asked. Why does Goneril "need" an hysterical exit line? Defiance has been her style since the end of the first scene of the play; hysteria appears nowhere else in her role. For that matter, is her exit in the Quarto version *necessarily* hysterical? Couldn't an actress say the speech grimly determined? Also, why *wouldn't* Albany first speak to Edmund and then return to the issue of his wife? Even if the Shakespearean usage of delayed responses is ignored, what evidence or prior condition might prevent Albany from following the sequence of events ascribed to him in the Folio? Does Albany display any consistent pattern of being a particularly fast-acting or even straight-thinking character throughout the play? Muir's third point about reconciling Edmund's two speeches in the Folio again fails to allow for alternative interpretations open to an actor in the role. "Ask me not what I know," need not be read defiantly. On Edmund's lips, the line may be a resigned admission of all guilt, meaning "You need not ask." His following speech could then continue in this somber mode. Edmund has not the will nor the strength to confess single crimes:

What you have charg'd me with,
That have I done,

And more, much more, the time will bring it out.
'Tis past, and so am I:
[Folio, 3121-24; 5.3.163-65]

A variant, in altering the speaker, may also change the *action* of the speech. As a dramatic script, either text may be supported with good reasons. Muir presents only one side of the argument.[8] The great danger in the discussion results from polemical stances which declare that one version is good and therefore the other must be wrong, corrupt, and non-Shakespearean. So many of the variants in *King Lear* present equally strong alternatives that it misrepresents the texts to speak of each choice as between one correct and one corrupt option. The internal logic and the internal dramatic development of the Quarto and the Folio may be ignored only at great risk of distorting the evidence for readers. This is particularly true of the major variants in this scene.

Although the next major variant eliminates seventeen lines in two speeches from Edgar's part and only one short speech from Albany's, paradoxically it is Albany's role that is most affected by the change. In both texts, Edgar narrates the tale of his "pilgrimage," ending his long speech with the report of his father's death. Judging from the responses of Edmund and Albany, this speech was meant to be extremely moving and important.

Bast. This speech of yours hath mov'd me,
And shall perchance do good, but speake you on,
You looke as you had something more to say.
Alb. If there be more, more wofull, hold it in,
For I am almost ready to dissolve,
Hearing of this.
[Folio, 3163-68; 5.3.200-205]

It must be noted that Edmund and Albany both respond strongly to Edgar's speech. But Edmund asks for more ("but speake you on"), while Albany says, in opposition, "hold it in." Edgar continues in the Quarto text, but immediately after Albany's speech in the Folio version Edgar's lines have been cut, leaving instead the entrance of the Gentleman who witnessed the deaths of Goneril and Regan. Albany's request, "hold it in," in its Quarto context has no consequence because Edgar goes on with his story. Not only does Albany fail to protest any further in the Quarto but he actually prompts Edgar later to reveal still more details. Thus, in the Quarto Albany's confession of emotional turmoil is not very important to the progress of the scene. His speech quoted above brings about or is part of no new dramatic action.

The context and the relative importance of Albany's appeal are altered by variants in the Folio. Edgar's following speech ("This would have seemd a periode . . ."), Albany's question to him, and Edgar's reply are all cut from the Folio. Instead of hearing more of Edgar's narrative, Albany receives a far greater shock immediately after he reveals how his emotions are precariously balanced. As with so many other variants in the Folio that affect Albany, the rhythm of events is accelerated by cutting lines from the Quarto version. Albany says "I am almost ready to dissolve, . . ." and the grisly sight of a man carrying a bloody knife appears before him. This quick succession of dramatic shocks for Albany is seen only in the Folio text; all composite versions follow the more discursive pattern of the Quarto.

Closely associated with Albany's expressed nervousness, the dialogue at the moment after the Gentleman's entrance is the next variant passage in the Folio. In the Quarto, however disturbed he may be, Albany is clearly in charge of the action:

> *Enter one with a bloudie knife,*
> *Gent.* Helpe, helpe,
> *Alb.* What kind of helpe, what meanes that bloudy knife?
> *Gent.* Its hot it smokes, it came even from the heart of-
> *Alb.* Who man, speake?
> *Gent.* Your Lady sir, your Lady, and her sister
> By her is poysoned, she hath confest it.
> [Quarto, L3; 5.3.222-28]

Albany is the only person to respond to the Gentleman's call for help. He alone asks all the questions. In the Folio, on the other hand, Edgar is the first to respond, and it is Edgar who questions the Gentleman coherently, although Albany's rough commands seem to get better results:

Alb. If there be more, more wofull, hold it in,
For I am almost ready to dissolve,
Hearing of this.
Enter a Gentleman.
Gen. Helpe, helpe: **O helpe.**
Edg. What kinde of helpe?
Alb. **Speake man.**
Edg. What meanes **this** bloody Knife?
Gen. 'Tis hot, it smoakes, it came even from the heart
of———**O she's dead.**
Alb. **Who dead? Speake man.**
Gen. Your Lady Sir, your Lady;
[Folio, 3166-77; 5.3.219-27; boldface indicates variants in Folio]

In its Folio context, Albany's earlier remark that he is ready to "dissolve" is followed at once by reinforcing and corroborating events. Albany's speeches and actions in the Folio are more in keeping with his statements about the emotional tension he feels.

Next, in quick succession, Albany hears about Goneril's and Regan's deaths, Kent returns to the stage and asks after Lear, Albany asks Edmund about Lear and Cordelia, and Albany and Kent turn to view the bodies of Goneril and Regan. The same events occur in both texts, but Albany's actions are presented differently. In the Folio, Albany responds distractedly, arhythmically; he is visibly distressed. In the Quarto text, which we shall examine first, he moves steadily from one emergent occasion to the next. He *says* he is emotionally tremulous, but he proceeds in an orderly, authoritative, and calm manner.

Alb. Produce their bodies, be they alive or dead,
This Justice of the heavens that makes us tremble,
Touches us not with pity.   *Edg.* Here comes Kent sir.
Alb. O tis he, the time will not allow   *Enter Kent*
The complement that very manners urges.
Kent. I am come to bid my King and maister ay good
night,
Is he not here?

> *Duke.* Great thing of us forgot,
> Speake Edmund, whers the king, and whers Cordelia
> Seest thou this object Kent.   *The bodies of Gonorill and*
> *Kent.* Alack why thus.   *Regan are brought in.*
> [Quarto, L3; 5.3.231-40]

A list of events from the Quarto text shows that Albany deals with each new event immediately as it occurs:

1. Albany commands that the bodies of Goneril and Regan be brought onto the stage.
2. He reports that the news of their deaths makes him tremble.
3. Edgar announces Kent's entrance.
4. Kent enters.
5. Albany reacts to Kent's entrance.
6. Kent asks for Lear.
7. Albany asks Edmund for the whereabouts of Lear and Cordelia.
8. Before Edmund responds, the bodies of Goneril and Regan are brought in.
9. Understandably distracted from his question about Lear and Cordelia, Albany calls Kent to view the bodies, which he himself sees now for the first time.

Albany's straightforward manner is thoroughly consistent with his behavior earlier in the Quarto when he responded to Goneril's exit and to the entrance of the Gentleman with the bloody knife.

The Folio reorders this sequence. The same words take on new meanings in altered contexts.

> *Edg.* Here comes Kent.
>   *Enter Kent.*
> *Alb.* Produce the bodies, be they alive or dead;
>   *Gonerill and Regans bodies brought out.*
> This judgement of the Heavens that makes us tremble.
> Touches us not with pitty: O, is this he?
> The time will not allow the complement
> Which very manners urges.
>   *Kent.* I am come

To bid my King and Master aye good night.
Is he not here?
   Alb. Great thing of us forgot,
Speake Edmund, where's the King? and where's Cordelia?
Seest thou this object Kent?
   Kent. Alacke, why thus?
                              [Folio, 3181-95; 5.3.230-40]

The Folio order shows Albany responding to clearly indicated events at odd and unexpected intervals, in sharp contrast to his orderly, timely reactions in the Quarto:

1. Edgar announces Kent's entrance (#3 in Quarto).
2. Kent enters (#4 in Quarto).
3. Albany commands that the bodies be brought out (#1 in Quarto).
4. The corpses are carried onto the stage (#8 in Quarto).
5. Albany reports that he is trembling. In this version the sight of the bodies, not just the news of the deaths, prompts Albany's reaction (#2 in Quarto).
6. Albany turns from the bodies to respond to Kent's entrance, four lines after it was announced (#5 in Quarto).

This is the Folio's second instance of Albany's disjointed reactions. (The first was his delayed response to Goneril's exit.)

7. Kent asks for Lear (#6 in Quarto).
8. Albany turns toward Edmund and questions him (#7 in Quarto).
9. Albany interrupts himself, before Edmund has a chance to reply to his questions, in order to call Kent's attention to the two bodies (#9 in Quarto).

This crucial contextual change is the third of Albany's discontinuous responses. Albany momentarily turns away from the issue of Lear and Cordelia in both texts. In the Quarto he is visibly motivated by the entrance of the bodies. But in the Folio Albany is prompted by some sudden eruption of concern within himself. The bodies have been onstage for ten lines.

In the Quarto version the audience's focus of attention

moves from Albany and his question about the king and Cordelia to the upstage doors and the bodies being carried in. Albany turns to watch, and he calls on Kent to turn as well. The Folio version directs the audience's attention differently. Ten lines *after* the audience first observes the bodies Albany makes his turn. Albany's action, not the entrance of the bodies, becomes the center of attention. (This same technique for controlling the focus of dramatic interest appears in the Folio version of Goneril's entrance in 2.4, where Lear responds after the event has been observed by the audience.) Albany's disjointed timing in the Folio here, like his delayed response to Goneril's exit and his belated notice of Kent's entrance, projects to the audience a clear signal reinforcing his words when he says, "I am almost ready to dissolve, / Hearing of this," and when he speaks of the "judgement of the Heavens that makes us tremble."

The significance of Albany's action itself should not pass unnoticed. This turn from Edmund to the bodies of Goneril and Regan marks the third time in the play that Albany retreats from considering the safety of Lear and Cordelia in order to deal with what seems to him a momentarily more important issue. First he had to ignore them in order to fight against the "enemy." After the "enemy" was defeated, Edmund's treasonous plot against his life occupied Albany while he suspended his demand for custody of Lear and Cordelia. And here, only a moment after he recognizes a "Great thing of us forgot," Albany again forgets. Albany only remembers Lear and Cordelia again nine lines later, when Edmund repeatedly insists that their danger is great and that haste is called for if they are to be saved.

> *Bast.* . . . Quickly send,
> (Be briefe in it) to'th'Castle, for my Writ
> Is on the life of Lear, and on Cordelia:
> Nay, send in time.
> [Folio, 3201-4; 5.3.245-48]

On each of three occasions in the plot, variants in the Folio center the audience's attention on Albany's choices and actions. Each time the audience is led to hope that Albany may act in some way to aid Lear and Cordelia. Each time Albany fails to act on their behalf. He does not try to help them and then fail; he simply does not try. Furthermore, the emergent occasions that prevent Albany's efforts to help Lear and Cordelia grow less and less compelling. An army of "invaders" seems a very strong motive to ignore the needs and safety of one's friends. The prosecution of Edmund for treason, after his army has been disbanded, seems significantly less urgent. And, finally, the presence of the dead as a reason to delay the rescue of the living seems least justifiable of all. As Howard Felperin observes, "Shakespeare in *King Lear* repeatedly holds out hope with his left hand only to take it back with his right; raises romantic expectations only to defeat them with tragic actualities. The play is full of false dawns."[9]

When Albany finally responds to the need to rescue Lear and Cordelia, he does not act in the resolute manner he displayed when he firmly established his own supremacy earlier in the scene. Instead he calls out an incoherent, effectively meaningless command:

> *Alb.* Run, run, O run.
> *Edg.* To who my Lord? Who ha's the Office?
> Send thy token of repreeve.
> [Folio, 3205-7; 5.3.248-50]

In the Quarto text, Albany recovers sufficiently to urge haste on the person carrying the token of authority, but in the Folio the speech is given to Edgar.

> *Bast.* Well thought on, take my Sword,
> Give it the Captaine.
> *Edg.* [*Duke* in Quarto] Hast thee for thy life.
> [Folio, 3208-10; 5.3.251-52]

The Folio variant serves again to leave Albany only the speech indicating his inner turmoil, removing the speech that in the Quarto indicates some degree of effective participation in the rescue effort.

Albany's last utterance in this section of the play has often been seen as one of Shakespeare's painful ironies indicative of the cruelties of the world. When read in the context of the

Folio variants, Albany's prayer, "The Gods defend her," throws a harsh light instead on his own repeated failures to defend Cordelia and Lear.

In the final section of the scene, after Lear's entrance, Albany has only five speeches in the Quarto text and only four in the Folio. The four speeches common to the Quarto and the Folio each declare Albany's emotional and physical withdrawal from the events before him. Albany's primary reaction to Lear's climactic return to the stage is quite unlike those of Kent and Edgar:

> *Kent.* Is this the promis'd end?
> *Edg.* Or image of that horror.
> *Alb.* Fall and cease.
> [Folio, 3224-26; 5.3. 264-65]

Kent and Edgar attempt to make some sense out of the event. In contrast, Albany's commands are an effort to obliterate somehow the image presented before him, perhaps by Lear's falling and ceasing, or perhaps by his own.[10]

Albany then remains silent for the following thirty-five lines. When he next speaks, Albany offers an explanation for his failure to address any further words to Lear:

> *Alb.* He knowes not what he saies, and vaine is it
> That we present us to him.
> [Folio, 3262-63; 5.3.294-95]

Albany may indeed be correct about Lear. Certainly Edgar agrees, replying "Very bootlesse." Nevertheless, it should be noted that throughout the scene, with the possible exception of his first outcry, "Fall and cease," Albany addresses *nothing* to Lear. Kent, Edgar, and the Gentleman (i.e., every other person who says anything at all up to this point) each either speak to or respond to the old king. Albany's speeches seem to be efforts to insulate himself from Lear.

Albany's third speech in this section of the scene attempts to set the kingdom aright, to restore Lear to a place of honor, and to distribute justice. He begins with a denigrating response to the news of Edmund's death:

> *Alb.* That's but a trifle heere:
> You Lords and Noble Friends, know our intent,
> What comfort to this great decay may come,
> Shall be appli'd. For us we will resigne,
> During the life of this old Majesty
> To him our absolute power, you to your rights,
> With boote, and such addition as your Honours
> Have more then merited. All Friends shall
> Taste the wages of their vertue, and all Foes
> The cup of their deservings. O see, see.
> [Folio, 3267-76; 5.3.296-305]

The "comfort" that Albany intends to apply to the kingdom is extremely disturbing. Although Lear is too weak and too confused even to be addressed directly by Albany in this speech, Albany nevertheless feels that it is somehow appropriate to restore to the king "our absolute power." In the first scene of the play, Lear gave away this power so that he might "Unburthen'd crawle toward death." He expected only "kindness" in return for his gift. While Albany gives Lear an unwanted burden of authority, he denies to him the least sign of filial affection.

Even stranger and less satisfying are Albany's promises to distribute rewards and punishments to friends and foes. Albany's categories of "friend" and "foe" are cruelly empty or confused. Excluding the nameless soldiers, everyone alive on the stage was Albany's foe in the battle just fought: King Lear, Kent, and Edgar. Albany's "friends," those who supported or encouraged his fight against the "enemy," all are dead: Cornwall, Goneril, Regan, Edmund, and Oswald. Albany is alone in the role of accuser. He offers no word of reconcilement, mercy, or healing pity for the "foes," whom he does not name.[11]

The last words of Albany's speech illuminate the inseparable fusion of Shakespeare's thoughts and his dramatic forms. In a passage found only in the Folio text of 4.6, Lear presented a philosophic critique of the kind of justice with which Albany is associated:

Place sinnes with Gold, and the strong Lance of Justice,
hurtlesse breakes: Arme it in ragges, a Pigmies straw do's
pierce it. None do's offend, none, I say none, Ile able
'em; take that of me my Friend, who have the power to
seale th'accusers lips.
[Folio, 2608-12; 4.6.165-70]

For Lear, conventional retribution as it is embodied in a harsh legal code, "the strong Lance of Justice," is nothing but an agency impotent against the powerful and devastating against the weak. Untempered by humility, the law's punishments are manifestations of the ruler's power rather than of his moral authority. A thousand lines after this passage inserted in the Folio, Albany stands before the king. The duke is an accuser who himself is suspiciously tainted by the crimes he intends to prosecute. The script does not indicate exactly how Lear accomplishes it, but some action he performs forces Albany to break off his sententious adjudications with the cry, "O see, see." Lear demonstrates with his dying breath that he does "have the power to seale th'accusers lips."

After Lear dies, Albany says nothing until he gives the command to remove the bodies of Lear and his three daughters, ten lines later. The shocking experience of Lear's final moments seems enough to prompt Albany to a second abdication. We cannot be sure why Albany disqualifies himself from further rule in the kingdom. We are not told. But certainly we should ask. Perhaps he perceives at Lear's death the ultimate consequences of his rigid code of justice, untempered by mercy, humility, or kindness, and the consequence of his failure to act with moral responsibility when he held the reins of power.

His first abdication was formal, carefully limited and conditioned, and part of his generalized impulse to be just: ". . . For us we will resigne / During the life of this old Majesty / To him our absolute power." For his second abdication, Albany's manner is totally transformed. His speech is vivid and simple. For the first time he allows himself to express the idea of unconditioned remorse. And his withdrawal from the exercise of power seems absolute:

> *Alb.* Beare them from hence, our present businesse
> Is generall woe: Friends of my soule, you twaine,
> Rule in this Realme, and the gor'd state sustaine.
>   [Folio, 3293-95; 5.3.319-21]

This second abdication does not imply, as does the first, that Albany intends to resume the throne later.

Finally, the only significant variant related to Albany in this section of the scene is the frequently discussed speech heading for the last speech in the play. It may be examined anew, in the light of the consistent patterns of characterization found in the two early texts. The two versions may then be seen as reasonable alternative conclusions to their respective texts. In the Quarto version, Albany delivers the last speech.

> *Duke.* The waight of this sad time we must obey,
> Speake what we feele, not what we ought to say,
> The oldest have borne most, we that are yong,
> Shall never see so much, nor live so long.
>   [Quarto, L4; 5.3.324-37]

This is perfectly consistent with Albany's characterization in the Quarto. His words indicate he has experienced a profound emotional event, but he acts as if he is still in complete control of himself and of the action. In the Quarto, Albany says that he gives the rule of the realm to Edgar and Kent, but he takes upon himself the responsibility of closing the scene. He says he abdicates, but we see him still in authority. According to the Quarto, Albany's second abdication seems suddenly inconclusive. This is not an unthinkable ending for *King Lear*.

The Folio text gives the last speech to Edgar. This change is consistent with other variants in the Folio increasing Edgar's role in the scene while reducing Albany's. Further, this final change in the Folio is consistent with the Folio's portrayal of Albany as a man whose actions are closely bound up with his emotions. Thus the ending in the Folio, with Albany withdrawing himself after he has expressed his need for mourning, seems highly appropriate to the Folio.

In summary, the variants in the Folio shape Albany's character in a number of complex ways. Clearly, his instincts are to act sympathetically toward Lear, but the Folio text amplifies the conflict in Albany between his humane instincts on the one hand and on the other his rigid principles of justice and his flaccid ethical practices. The foregoing analysis has stressed the negative qualities of Albany's characterization in the play simply because they have so often been completely discounted by commentators. It must always be admitted that Albany is indeed a sympathetic figure in *King Lear*. But the ambiguities created by changes in the Folio must not be ignored. Edgar refers to Albany as Goneril's "vertuous Husband," but the Folio adds Kent's lines about "the hard Reine which both" Albany and Cornwall bear against Lear. Albany condemns his wife's atrocious mistreatment of her father, but he utterly fails to intercede on Lear's behalf on three separate occasions. Albany's good will toward Lear and Cordelia is not to be questioned, but his actions reported and shown on the stage, particularly in the Folio, repeatedly point up the disparities between his impulses and his deeds.

The final scene is the most important for Albany. Variants in the Folio text of this scene amplify Albany's performance as a vigorous prosecutor of treason committed against himself. Further variants create for him in the Folio a series of disjointed actions that give credence to his remarks about his own state of inner turmoil. The display of emotional tension in the Folio makes Albany's second abdication at the end of the scene justifiable, because Albany's need to withdraw from active life has been shown so convincingly. In contrast, Albany's statements about his inner crises are not very compelling in the Quarto, since they have no consequence or observable counterpart in his actions. Therefore his second abdication may be interpreted as inconclusive, especially considering the Quarto's ascription of the final speech. In both texts Albany is a complex and ambiguous figure. His intentions are not commensurate with his actions and their consequences.

This reading of Albany's character in *King Lear* is utterly and irreconcilably at odds with the conventional view. In part because of the universal acceptance of the modern composite version of the play, in part from a consistent but inexplicable discounting of the events in the play, almost all critics speak of Albany as one of Shakespeare's paragons.[12] A representative selection of opinions about Albany yields these characterizations of his role: he is a practically flawless "measuring figure of decency"; a "great man, great in psychological strength, great in physical power, great in speech, great in piety and morality"; he is one of "Shakespeare's gentlest characters"; and at the end of the play he is seen as "the only major figure in *King Lear* who loses neither moral rectitude nor high temporal position."[13] This last comment is found in slightly different formulations in many critical analyses of Albany; for example, in this recent statement: "Deep in his wife's shadow during most of the play, Albany at last shines with the strength and knowledge that the tragedy has allowed him to acquire. He finally proves himself to be his wife's master and master of his realm. When order returns, he strengthens it by becoming what he never was."[14] Concerning Albany's final status in the play, another critic speaks of Edmund's trial as a ritual "which restores Edgar to status and inheritance, eliminates Edmund, and leaves the political field clear for Albany at last." Yet again, another critic is able to reason as follows: "Receiver of the kingdom as the highest ranking survivor, Albany, like other figures in the final sequence, thus attains his identity."[15] These interpretations of Albany's character and his development are nothing less than wrong. They somehow ignore the full testimony of the play, either in the Quarto, the Folio, or the modern versions.

Readers of *King Lear* believe that Albany is simple and honest and good because he proclaims his own innocence on several occasions, because he is outraged by Gloucester's blinding, because he defends Britain against "foreign invasion," and because he presides over the trial that brings Edmund to justice. But not one of these virtuous acts is presented unequivocally by Shakespeare. Each is the locus of significant variants. Despite his virtue, Albany is censured as Cornwall's partner by Kent and then by Lear. Despite his outrage, Albany does nothing to relieve either Gloucester, Lear, or Cordelia. Despite his conquest of the "enemy," his defense of Britain is shown in its consequences to be a tragic blunder.

And finally, Albany's needless urgency to try Edmund leads him to ignore the danger to Lear and Cordelia, a negligence that contributes directly to their deaths. Albany is indeed a good man, just as Brutus is a good man; but like Brutus, Albany makes choices leading to tragedy.

CHAPTER VI

Contemporary Bibliographical Theories and Editorial Practices and the Case for Authorial Revision

> Bibliographical work is fascinating for him who happens to be afflicted with the disease. It is stupid work in the eyes of him who is not, but it becomes useful work in the eyes of even the scoffers if circumstances compel them to depend upon a piece of bibliographic work well done.
> Oscar George Theodore Sonneck, 1916[1]

For the major variants in the Folio version of *King Lear*, only one explanation does not require the acceptance of hypotheses that are either demonstrably false or so complex as to be patently improbable. This explanation is that the Quarto was printed from Shakespeare's foul papers, and the Folio was printed from the Quarto version that was carefully brought into agreement with the official promptbook. The promptbook itself embodied all of Shakespeare's own revisions, including additions, cuts, substitutions, and rearrangements. The Quarto and Folio do not represent two partial copies of a single original, but instead they are different stages of a composition, an early and a final draft. Except for only a very few variants that are obviously the result of errors in copying or printing, the vast majority of the changes found in the Folio must be accepted as Shakespeare's final decisions. The modern practice of printing a composite text eclectically chosen from the Quarto and Folio seriously distorts Shakespeare's most profound play.

I contend that all the objections raised against the theory of revision must be discounted on the basis of widely observed and accepted evidence found in the Shakespeare canon. Furthermore, no other theory that has been proposed can account for the observed data without violating the facts, logic, or the known practices of theater artists of Shakespeare's time.

First, it will be necessary to establish that the Quarto is genuinely Shakespeare's and not a corruption embodying heavy overlays of contaminated scribal interference. And next, the plausibility of Shakespeare as an artist who is capable of revising his own work must be confirmed.

W. W. Greg and Alice Walker raise the strongest objections to taking the Quarto text as a direct copy of the author's foul papers.[2] And although specific details of their arguments may be rejected by contemporary editors, all modern editions nevertheless appear to be derived from these two scholars' work. Greg and Walker argue that the original manuscript that was used as copy for the Quarto could not have been a Shakespearean autograph for the following reasons (their arguments and the specific examples they cite in support of their claims will be discussed at greater length):

1. The Quarto contains many obviously corrupt passages.
2. The Quarto misassigns speeches and adapts them to wrong speakers.
3. The Quarto has many "anomalous" spellings, unlikely to be of Shakespearean origin, some of which are "grotesque mishearings."
4. The Quarto is punctuated very poorly.
5. The Quarto prints much verse as prose, prose as verse, and mislines much verse.
6. Miss Walker finds much evidence of "memorial error," of a type not likely to have resulted from a compositor's work on the setting of authorial foul papers.

"Obviously corrupt passages" imply that the copy used was indecipherable to the compositor of the Quarto. Shakespeare's hand in the *Sir Thomas More* manuscript is at times, by Greg's testimony, "sometimes obscure" and "indecipherble."[3] Greg also reasons that the manuscript used to set the Second Quarto of *Hamlet*, thought to be Shakespeare's foul papers, must have been "difficult" for the compositor to decipher, and contained "tangles of Shakespeare's" own writing (*First Folio*, pp. 312-14). So "corruption" found in the *Lear* Quarto may *support* the possibility that Shakespeare's foul papers were used as copy. But certainly "corruption" or obscurity of meaning may not rule out the foul papers as copy.

Greg also claims that many speeches are misassigned in the Quarto (*First Folio*, p. 378). His prime example is 5.3.81, TLN 3026, where Regan, in the Folio, says, "Let the Drum strike, and prove my title thine." Greg argues that this "appears absurdly perverted and misassigned in Q as 'Bast. Let the drum strike, and prove my title good.'" But there is nothing at all absurd about the Quarto's reading. Greg confuses readings that are merely different with those that are wrong. The Quarto actually has not a single speech heading that might be considered "wrong." At no point, for example, does Goneril have a line which would properly make sense only in Lear's part. We never find a speech given to a character who is not onstage. In fact, as Chapter 5 of this study demonstrates, the Quarto handles many dialogues in ways perfectly consistent with itself, and the Folio makes several rather consistent kinds of changes. Such a pattern of variation again supports, rather than challenges, the Quarto's status as an authorial draft.

Two varieties of spelling irregularity are offered by Greg and Walker as evidence that the copy used to set up the Quarto was not a Shakespearean autograph. Spellings "unlikely to have been of Shakespearean origin" noted by Walker include "cushings" for "cushions," "so phisticated," for "sophisticated," and "in sight" for "incite." Walker states, "There is no reason for supposing that Shakespeare's spelling was uninstructed," and she infers from the evidence of the spelling and from the evidence of verse lining (discussed below) that "the manuscript from which the Quarto was printed was taken down by dictation" (*Textual Problems*, pp. 40-44). Greg also concludes that several strangely spelled words and phrases are the result of a copyist writing from dictation. He labels as "grotesque mishearings" the Quarto readings of "in sight" for "incite," and "a dogge, so bade in office" for "a dog's obeyed in office" (*First Folio*, p. 378).

The testimony of the examples cited by Greg and Walker yet again strengthens the case in favor of Shakespearean copy for the Quarto rather than argues against it. First, the pages generally accepted as being in Shakespeare's hand in *Sir Thomas More* demonstrate that his spelling is worse than "uninstructed," it is positively aggressive in its inconsistency and abhorrence of rule. J. Dover Wilson remarks: "The spellings of the Addition [i.e., the Shakespearean pages] look uncouth, if not illiterate, to a modern eye unaccustomed to read sixteenth century manuscripts.... Then a gentleman spelt as he list, and only 'base mechanicals' such as compositors spelt more or less consistently."[4] Second, Greg confirms that the Second Quarto of *Hamlet*, likely derived from Shakespeare's foul papers, "swarms with abnormal spellings" (*First Folio*, p. 313). Third, Wilson lists a number of spelling habits common to both the Shakespearean hand in *Sir Thomas More* and the *Lear* Quarto, for example the doubled final consonants, "dogge" and "gotte," and the frequent absence of the mute final "e," such as "don" for "done." Fourth, the sample of Shakespeare's writing in *Sir Thomas More* contains a peculiarity that, without resorting to hypothetical readers and transcribers, explains some of the errors Greg labelled as "grotesque mishearings." The following appear in the Shakespearean autograph passage: "fo rbid" (line 96), "o ffyc" (line 98), "th offendo r" (line 123), and "count ry" (line 126).[5] "So phisticated" from the Quarto is anomalous, as Walker declares it to be, but it is a very Shakespearean anomaly.

Greg fails to recognize that the difference between "a dogge, so bade in office" from the Quarto and "a dog's obeyed in office" is more likely caused by graphical confusion (i.e., related to the written forms of the words) rather than phonetic error during dictation (caused by similarity of sounds). The two versions have distinct speech stresses and pauses and distinguishable consonant sounds when read aloud. In the "correct" Folio reading, the " 's" at the end of "dog's" is an elision of "is," and it is pronounced as a "z." The "o" in "obeyed" is not a stressed vowel. The copyist would have had to "mishear" an "s" for a "z" and also mishear a stress and hear momentary pauses before and after "so" in order to get "Ă dógg, só báde in óffĭce" from what the reader presumably pronounced as "Ă dóg'z ŏbéyed ĭn óffĭce." Although this is not impossible, it seems highly suspicious that such an odd pattern of mishearing "s" for "z" and hearing inappropriately stressed syllables and unpronounced speech pauses does not occur at any other point in the Quarto text. All the other "mishearings" claimed by Greg and Walker each require unique mishearings of different kinds of sounds.

Two kinds of graphic confusion, one related to Shakespeare's handwriting and one to the Quarto compositor's quirks of punctuation, perhaps may be more likely sources for the reading "a dogg, so bade in office." (I offer this explanation very tentatively, only to show there are other hypotheses to be considered.) The hand thought to be Shakespeare's in *Sir Thomas More* occasionally left long spaces between adjacent letters of single words, as in "fo rbid" and "offendo r." Also, the Quarto compositor occasionally inserted commas in odd places, sometimes in apparent attempts to make sense out of confusion in his copy. (For example, we find "bould in the quarrels, rights" [Quarto, D4; 2.1.54] and "his notion, weaknes" [Quarto, D1^v; 1.4.228] where the Folio reads "Bold in the quarrels right" [TLN 990] and "his Notion weakens" [TLN 741]. The comma after "notion" in the Quarto could be a compositor's or perhaps proofreader's workmanlike solution to a graphic puzzle if the copy before him read "his notion weaknes.") So, seeking an explanation more satisfying than mishearing, I offer that the manuscript copy had something like "a dogges o bade in office." The compositor may have joined the detached "o" to the preceding rather than to the following letter grouping, producing "a doggeso bade in office," and then a comma was inserted after "dogge," leaving us finally with "a dogge, so bade in office."

Such an interpretation of the source of error has the distinct advantage that it is consonant with other observed instances of manuscript and compositorial practice. It does not require the intervention of hypothetical agents whose characteristics must be deduced only from the few variants under investigation and which appear nowhere else.

An explanation less exotic than surreptitious dictation can account for the Quarto text's "mishearing" of "in sight" for "incite." First, Elizabethans were comfortable writing "a leven" for "eleven": "in sight" may be a similar usage. But a stronger case may be made. "In sight" appears as one of the rhyming words in an exit-couplet, Cordelia's last speech in 4.4:

> No blowne ambition doth our armes in sight
> But love, deere love, and our ag'd fathers right,
> Soone may I heare and see him.   *Exit.*
> [Quarto, I1^v; 4.4.27-29]

In its poetic context, the mishearing turns out to be an instance of eye-rhyming. In fact, the Folio prints the rhyming words as "incite" and "Rite." The Quarto and Folio spellings seem much more likely to be products of the poet or the compositor than the products of dictation and mishearing.[6]

In his own discussion of handwriting, Greg suggests a further reason to discount the theory that a dictated scribal copy of the foul papers intervened between the original and the Quarto: "If we find any considerable number of eccentric or archaic spellings in a print, the likelihood is great that it was set up from the author's own manuscript and not from a scribal copy" (*First Folio*, p. 148). As if in response to such an objection, Walker adds the further hypothetical condition on her scribes that they could not have been writers "professionally (in any sense)" (*Textual Problems*, p. 42). Since they were not professionals, she implies, they were therefore not "normalizing" spellers.

However, far greater restraints than these are placed upon the acceptability of a theory of transcription by dictation. R.W.B. McKerrow lists examples of errors in other printed texts that could only have resulted from dictation. They in no way resemble any of those errors in the *Lear* Quarto that Greg and Walker claim are the result of dictation. More important, one of the unavoidable consequences of working from dictation, McKerrow observes, is that the spelling in the original manuscript *"could have no influence whatever"* upon the copy being made.[7] Only the reader would see the graphic forms of the words in the original. But the Quarto of *King Lear* contains many spellings and graphic forms that are decidedly Shakespearean. Greg himself, although he fails to recognize that his observation invalidates the theory of dictation, suggests: "Q has 'Gonorill' throughout, F 'Gonerill.' Since 'Gonorill' is the form in the source-play of *King Leir*, this may have been Shakespeare's spelling, the change being made in the prompt-book. Even the spelling 'Leir' persists occasionally in Q, where it is more likely to be due to Shakespeare than to the compositor" (*First Folio*, pp. 385-86). The process of dictation hypothesized by Walker simply could not have yielded the Shakespearean spellings and other Shakespearean oddities observed in the Quarto.

The next objection to the Quarto as a copy of Shakespeare's foul papers is that the Quarto's punctuation is very light and sometimes misleading. It is heavier, however, and more helpful as rhetorical pointing than the punctuation of the Shakespearean pages in *Sir Thomas More*. And it is heavier than (and much in the style of) the punctuation found in the Second Quarto of *Hamlet*. Again, the relative lack of punctuation in the *Lear* Quarto may not be used as evidence *against* the Quarto's being drawn from an authorial manuscript, because the Quarto punctuation in fact resembles Shakespeare's.

The more difficult problem of mislined verse, sometimes set as prose in the Quarto and sometimes oddly divided, has frequently baffled critics, and it has prompted many ingenious explanations. Walker postulates that the true Shakespearean foul papers were lined just like the Folio version. She reasons that the misalignment in the Quarto results from a process of dictation and transcription of the foul papers that produced an intermediate text. This derivative text was then used as the copy for the Quarto (*Textual Problems*, pp. 42-43). Walker and Greg further explain that at certain times the copyists must have carefully indicated the proper line-endings, but at other times either the compositor of the Quarto had to guess at the line divisions himself, yielding "erroneous" lineation, or he simply printed his undivided copy as prose. The copyists' lineation efforts must have been quite inconsistently applied while they worked, since some scenes are partly in perfect alignment and partly mislined.

Misalignment may also be explained, however, without resorting to the hypothesis of dictation. The text of *Timon of Athens* contains many of the same verse-lining characteristics found in the Quarto text of *Lear*. E. K. Chambers says of *Timon*: "There is much mislineation in the text. Lines are irregularly divided; prose speeches are printed as verse, and verse speeches as prose.... Many lines are split, and the splitting is often not explicable as due to considerations of space or a desire to indicate major pauses. It is very likely that there were frequent marginal insertions in the copy."[8] Fredson Bowers interprets these findings to mean that "*Timon* cannot be regarded as suitable for acting; but there is no reason to suppose that it is not representative of Shakespeare in the workshop."[9] Greg concurs that "there is, of course, no doubt that F was printed from foul papers that had never been reduced to anything like order" (*First Folio*, p. 411).

A pattern of "irregularity" in the verse lining of *Timon* is noted by J. C. Maxwell, the editor of the New [Cambridge] Shakespeare: "At first sight, the lineation of *Timon* appears very defective, but closer examination suggests that the compositor probably made quite a good job of interpreting his copy.... There are few errors in lineation in passages of verse that is clearly intended to be regular.... In some of the rougher scenes, Shakespeare had probably not decided exactly what was to be verse and what prose."[10] The same suggestion suits the more numerous and extensive mislined passages in the Quarto text of *King Lear*. Maxwell's proposal about *Timon* has the great advantage of accounting for the large number of lines in *Lear*, over half the total in verse, which are divided correctly.[11] Once more, the evidence supports a view that the *Lear* Quarto was drawn directly from Shakespeare's foul papers rather than from an intermediate document.

The most widely accepted aspect of Walker's hypothesis among editors of *Lear* is her proposal that the Quarto differs from the genuine Shakespearean foul papers because the agents involved in dictating and writing their surreptitious copy introduced what she calls "memorial contamination." This is part of an extraordinarily complicated scenario that seems to have captured the imaginations of editors and textual critics. Yet it is possible to demonstrate that this final link in Walker's chain of inferences and hypotheses is without basis in the text of *Lear*.

First, the definition of "memorial error" or "memorial contamination" has a very cloudy and shifting history in textual studies. Before Duthie and others demonstrated that transcription from actual performance was not a possible way of producing a text of a play, memorial errors were those variant words, found in texts thought to have been "pirated" by stenographers, which supposedly reflected an actor's alteration of his part during performance. Thus "actor's gag" or "actor's vulgarizations" were blamed for what were felt to be un-Shakespearean phrases, words, expletives, or interjections. But E. K. Chambers argues that without stenographic reporting, such performers' lapses could not ordinarily find their way into a written text (*Facts and Problems*, I, 235n). Another much more limited definition of memorial error has been frequently applied in textual studies. If a copyist or compositor reads at one glance a very long string of words and holds it in his mind while he sets the words in type or writes them out, it is quite common for one word to be substituted for another of equivalent meaning, or size, or shape, or grammatical function. However, there are some limits to the number and kind of such memorial errors. Where, for example, a compositor's copy and the text he produces can be compared, the standards of accuracy are not extraordinarily high, but they are quite good. One study showed that a compositor reprinting *Richard II* (in 1598) committed on an average of once in every seventeen lines an error "of a memorial nature.... He frequently substituted one word for another, interpolated or omitted a word. The words thus affected are not usually nouns and verbs but instead are connectives and qualifiers (conjunctions, prepositions, articles, pronouns, and less frequently, adjectives and adverbs)."[12] This kind of memorial error is nothing like that formerly linked to transcriptions of performances, nor is it like the vast majority of variant readings found in the Quarto of *King Lear*.

The "memorial contamination" proposed by Walker is quite different from either the earlier usage of the term or the more restricted definition applied to copyists and compositors. Walker presumes that the two pirates had before them the foul papers, which differed only slightly from the promptbook and which were "surreptitiously dictated to a scribe by an actor who, for some reason we can only guess at (haste, over-confidence, laziness, inattention) relied on his memory instead of his script for the dialogue with which he was familiar. The contaminating actor-reader was, I judge, a small-part actor, probably the boy who played Goneril. The scribe may have been an actor too. The memorial contamination is certainly heaviest in scenes involving both Goneril and Regan" (*Textual Problems*, p. 41).

To illustrate what she means by a memorially contaminated passage, Walker quotes the Folio version of Lear's first long speech in the first scene, italicizing words that are different in the Quarto. Then she lists the Quarto and the Folio equivalents side by side for comparison. Beneath the list she writes: "The quarto also omits seven lines. *Not all these errors are necessarily memorial, but some of them certainly are* and the speech reflects no credit on the corrupter. . . . I do not think that the corruption is [Burbage's]: the readings are too poor, and the corruption is more likely to have been that of a less accomplished actor who had played some other part in the scene and had only a confused recollection of Lear's lines" (*Textual Problems*, pp. 44-45, my italics). Greg warns that the major requirement for accepting Walker's hypothesis is that "we must, to begin with, be confident that we can clearly distinguish between memorial contamination and other forms of corruption, and of this it may be easier to convince ourselves than others" (*First Folio*, p. 382). But Walker herself is unwilling to identify any specific instances of memorial corruption.

Two insurmountable barriers stand between Walker's hypothesis and normal probability. First, there is no valid reason and no known precedent which leads us to suppose that a reader would abandon the text before his eyes and instead rely on his memory for long passages.[13] This is particularly a problem because it is an unlikely procedure, especially in passages of rapid dialogue like those in the scenes that Walker claims are most memorially contaminated. Second, Walker's thesis requires that the "reader" was capable of reeling off complex dialogue so different from the copy before his eyes and so different from what the players were supposed to say that his work amounts to extempore playwriting. Although the hypothetical "reader's" memory was not very good, his capacity to turn out Shakespearean verse and prose different from the copy in the foul papers, frequently in perfectly rhythmic lines, is astounding. In the three most "contaminated" scenes, 1.1, 2.4, and 5.3, modern editors consistently choose many of the "reader's memorial contaminations" in preference to Shakespeare's "original" as reported in the Folio. Walker claims, for example, that memorial error is responsible for the Quarto's rendering of the action after Edmund falls in 5.3: "All the dialogue hereabouts in 5.3 is, in fact, very poor text. The interchange between Goneril and Albany after Edmund's defeat is as slovenly as much of 1.1" (*Textual Problems*, p. 46). But most editors actually prefer many aspects of the Quarto's "slovenly memorial reconstruction," produced by Walker's hypothetical reader, over the "Shakespearean" version of this passage in the Folio. Walker argues for "memorial contamination" produced by an actor who, in an attempt to remember what he heard on stage, can spontaneously "dictate" or "recall" prose and verse dialogue that would be virtually indistinguishable from Shakespeare's if we did not have a better text of *King Lear* in the Folio.

When the details of the Quarto text are seen in a larger context of Shakespearean textual data, it is not very difficult to identify the agent responsible for the copy used to set up the Quarto. When the confusing hypotheses are set aside and the observable facts are examined by themselves it is found that the person (or persons) who wrote the Quarto's copy had these characteristics:

1. His spelling was just like Shakespeare's.
2. His handwriting evidently displayed the same kinds of oddities as Shakespeare's.
3. He could at times write out by ear perfectly divided Shake-

spearean lines of the most complex rhythmic design without errors in words, stresses, or lineation, and at other times he could write verse as prose and prose as verse, in an uncanny resemblance to the patterns found in the copy for *Timon of Athens*.
4. He could change dialogue from one complex and meaningful pattern to another slightly less complex but still quite meaningful pattern, so quickly and so effortlessly that he did not need to consult the "original" text lying before him.
5. He could "corrupt" Shakespearean expressions with "vulgar" equivalents from the stage or from his faulty memory, but on occasion either his corruption or his transmission was "better" or "more Shakespearean" than the version found in the Folio text.

The agent most likely to have produced the spelling, spacing, lineation, textual illegibility, verbal structures, patterns of dialogue, and dramatic designs in the Quarto of *King Lear* is Shakespeare himself. The testimony of the pages from *Sir Thomas More*, the text of *Timon of Athens*, and the Second Quarto of *Hamlet* contradicts every point in Walker's hypotheses. However attractive the scenario of two boys "yarking up" a surreptitious transcript might be, it requires such a suspension of probable cause and the strenuous omission of so much evidence from the body of known Shakespearean practice that it should therefore be dismissed in its entirety.

Since the alternative theories attempting to account for the copy behind the Quarto text have also been proven inadequate or have been withdrawn by those who proposed them, the sole remaining possibility is that the copy was Shakespeare's foul-paper manuscript itself.

Before discussing the possibility that Shakespeare himself revised *King Lear*, it is necessary to recount modern opinions about whether Shakespeare revised any of his work at all. This is an extremely sensitive issue. The case of E. K. Chambers, for example, demonstrates how one very influential critic may have several quite contradictory opinions about Shakespeare's manner of composition. To the question, "Did he himself alter or rewrite what he at first composed?" (*Facts and Problems*, 1, 94), Chambers offers different answers. He suggests that Shakespeare did not himself make theatrical cuts, in which "two or three hundred lines go, to prevent normal [time] limits from being exceeded, or merely to prevent particular scenes or speeches from dragging. Probably *Hamlet* was always too long for performance as a whole. Shakespeare may have been more intent upon his poetry than upon getting it over the stage-rails. One hopes that he remained unperturbed when some of his best lines were sacrificed" (*Facts and Problems*, 1, 229). Chambers grudgingly admits that some evidence from Shakespearean texts "indicates revision, no doubt, in a sense, but by no means necessarily the wholesale revision of a play. The alterations may be mere afterthoughts at the time of original composition. We cannot ... take quite literally the statement of Heminges and Condell that they had scarce received a blot in Shakespeare's papers. It would be absurd to take it quite literally. But it certainly does not suggest any constant habit of self-revision" (*Facts and Problems*, 1, 232). Indeed, for such complex textual cases as those in *Hamlet, Troilus and Cressida, Othello,* and *King Lear*, Chambers discounts any possibility of Shakespearean revision as a source of alternative readings. For instance, in Chambers's view, the Second Quarto of *Hamlet* "substantially represents the original text of the play, as written once and for all by Shakespeare" (*Facts and Problems*, 1, 412). When he discusses Shakespeare's hand in the play of *Sir Thomas More*, however, Chambers alters his opinion about the playwright's "habit of self-revision":

> What one does not find is that absence of "blots" for which Heminges and Condell especially lauded Shakespeare. There are a score of places which show alterations made either *currente calamo* or as afterthoughts. And even then there were some oversights left for Hand C to correct. Perhaps the writer did not take the play he was tinkering very seriously. I do not take the statement of Heminges and Condell very seriously. If the scene is Shakespeare's, we get some useful hints towards the interpretation of the Quarto and Folio texts.
> [*Facts and Problems*, 1, 509]

Unfortunately, Chambers applies none of the insights gained from the Shakespearean autograph back to his discussions of the plays themselves, where Shakespeare clearly was working on matter that he took very seriously.

W. W. Greg finds some evidence of very limited Shakespearean revision between the Second Quarto and the Folio versions of *Hamlet*, between the Quarto and the Folio versions of *2 Henry IV*, and in isolated parts of other texts as well. Greg imaginatively reconstructs the derivation of the two texts of *Troilus and Cressida*, portraying Shakespeare as an artist who may freely revise in the course of rewriting or simply copying out one of his plays. While he was making a new copy of *Troilus*, Greg proposes, "Shakespeare wrote from the foul papers himself, observing of course his alterations, but making inevitably many small changes in the text. Whenever he was dissatisfied with an expression he doubtless altered it if on the spur of the moment he could devise a better; but most of the changes were probably unconscious, and he may even have made occasional errors and omissions" (*First Folio*, pp. 347-48). And in Greg's discussion of *Othello*, he surmises that behind the Quarto and Folio texts there was the author's "much and carelessly altered foul papers," or perhaps even a manuscript with "alterations made by the author or with his authority after his draft had been officially copied" (p. 369).

Fredson Bowers also states his belief in Shakespeare's possible activity as a revising writer. Generally, Bowers says, "few authors can resist the opportunity to revise during the course of copying," and more particularly, "I am not so convinced as some critics that the perfection of Shakespeare's plays was achieved in only a single act of composition" (*On Editing Shakespeare*, pp. 19, 107). A further observation of his is quite valuable in pinpointing the source of critical resistance to the idea that Shakespeare created most of the variants in the text of *Lear*: "Shakespeare is obviously not so costive as Ben Jonson but his rate of production does not preclude various stages of drafting and revision in papers that could scarcely be given to the company. I am far from sure that the common view is not still subtly influenced by the concept of Shakespeare as Fancy's child, warbling his native woodnotes wild" (*On Editing Shakespeare*, p. 26).

Indeed, the high expectations commonly held by critics about the quality of Shakespeare's early drafts are without foundation in any evidence. The expectations are strongly contradicted by the text of *Timon* and by variants admitted to be authorial in plays with good quartos, particularly *Hamlet, Othello*, and *Troilus and Cressida*. Nevertheless, the critic's assumptions about Shakespeare's "unblotted papers" are the perennial justification for rejecting the two texts of *Lear* as possible stages in Shakespeare's work on the play. Madeleine Doran rejects her own early theory of the Shakespearean revision in *Lear* because she cannot believe that Shakespeare could write unformed or inchoate verse as it appears in the *Lear* Quarto.[14] Greg rejects the possibility of revision in *Lear* because he doubts that Shakespeare, "at the height of his powers, could ever have written the clumsy and fumbling lines we find in Q, or that these could in general represent a stage in the development of F."[15] Duthie rejects authorial revision in *Lear* because he does not think that Shakespeare would make so many single-word substitutions in the course of rewriting, "without any incorporation of new structures or new ideas."[16] And Muir rejects the possibility of authorial revision because he feels that the hypothetical "original" text, made up of all the lines from the Quarto and the Folio, is so superior to the cut text in the Folio that the Folio revision could only have been made by the company after Shakespeare's death.[17] These views, although held by reputable bibliographers, are nevertheless based on conjecture and not upon evidence. The extant evidence from *Sir Thomas More, Timon of Athens, Othello,* and *Troilus and Cressida* indicates that Shakespeare's early thoughts could possibly be quite rough, subject to minute and seemingly unmotivated substitution of synonymous words, and liable to heavy recasting in shorter or longer forms.[18]

As a corollary to the unrealistic expectations critics hold about Shakespeare's spontaneous perfection in composing *King Lear*, they also erroneously see the passage of Shakespeare's text into the playhouse as an inevitable and unfortunate desecration. The process of "theatrical adaptation" or "theatrical cutting" is universally described as a destructive assault, carried out by persons whose interests are alien to the author's artistic concerns, and especially hostile to his script. Theobald was the first editor to assume that the actors altered the text of *King Lear* to suit their own fancy, without the knowledge or consent of the playwright. Although we now know much more about how the acting companies of the period worked, Theobald's view still exerts an influence disproportionate to its worth. For example, G. Blakemore Evans vividly illustrates the modern view of "theatrical cutting" in *King Lear*:

> One substantial passage, a whole scene (4.3), occurs only in Q1-2, and in such a case the editor is forced to judge its authenticity on its own merits, without the aid of immediate context. The poetic quality and general context of the scene are such, however, that no editor, since Pope first included it in an edited text, has seriously questioned its Shakespearean origin. *It is, moreover, the kind of scene that can be deleted without any dislocation of the plot-line, hence a natural prey for a book-keeper intent on shortening an overlong play.* [*The Riverside Shakespeare*, p. 37; my italics]

Like Alice Walker's scenario of Goneril and the pirates, the image conjured up by Evans has a distinct, imaginative appeal. As soon as Shakespeare's back is turned, the predatory bookkeeper ravenously despoils the hitherto unblotted papers in order to shorten *King Lear* by four minutes. Theatrical cutting of altogether three hundred lines, the actual reduction of the Folio, would save about twenty minutes of playing time.

Three debilitating errors are committed by reasoning such as Evans's. The first is the matter of actions and motives attributed to the bookkeeper in the playhouse. There are twelve marked promptbooks from the period that show the kinds of changes made on a script by a prompter or bookkeeper. Greg, the most competent authority on these playhouse documents, concludes that plays were never cut because they were too long:

> The cuts make no great impression on the length of the play and appear to have been usually made on what may be called local grounds, to remove offence or obscurity,

to lighten over-long speeches, or for other mainly literary reasons. There is little indication of a desire to reduce plays to a standard length. It may be true that, Shakespeare and Jonson apart, the average length of plays of the period was about 2,400 lines and the usual length of performance some two hours. But there are allusions to plays lasting two and a half and even three hours, and the promptbook of *Believe as you List* was not cut though it runs over 3,000 lines: *Ironside*, which is not much over 2,000 lines, is more heavily cut than *Woodstock*, which is about 3,000. On the evidence we are bound to believe that plays differed considerably in length and performances in duration. [*First Folio*, pp. 146-47]

The cuts in the Folio version of *King Lear* do not essentially resemble those in the extent promptbooks, nor were the promptbooks apparently cut in order to save playing time. The cuts in *King Lear*, as I have demonstrated, reflect artistic revision rather than mechanical care about playing time.

The second error committed by Evans and most modern editors is to assume that if a passage is recognizably Shakespearean then it must ipso facto be included in the printed text. Shakespeare was a very fluent writer. It is quite conceivable that he wrote material which he later decided was excessive, and then he cut it himself. Evans implies that only other hands would cut lines from Shakespeare's play after he had completed his "original" draft. But it is not enough to determine that Shakespeare wrote a line which was left out of the Folio text. It must also be demonstrated that some other agent, not Shakespeare, made the cut. My analysis of the two texts has shown that more Shakespeare is not necessarily better Shakespeare. There is no compelling reason for reinserting cut lines automatically.

Third, and most important, the idea of destructive theatrical cutting seriously violates everything we know about Shakespeare's life as an artist intimately involved in every aspect of theatrical production. Working with the foremost company of his time, Shakespeare was the company's main playwright, one of its leading actors and, as a shareholder, an active participant in all its ventures. Probably the greatest sources of his artistic fecundity and confidence were his daily association with the players in his company and his performances with them throughout his productive life. Therefore, while bibliographic analysis reveals that theatrical cuts were indeed made in preparing *King Lear*, it is equally apparent that theatrical additions were made as well. And it is unreasonable to declare that "theatrical" cuts, changes, or additions were made without the active involvement of Shakespeare himself as part of the creative process in preparing the play for the stage. *King Lear* is not a drama composed by a fledgling poet in his study; it is perhaps the most theatrical tragedy written by the world's foremost playwright, who had acted in scores of plays and written at least twenty-five for his own theater to be performed by his friends and by himself. One must wonder what kinds of cuts Shakespeare could conceivably make in a script he was working on if they were not to be "theatrical" cuts.

Alternative explanations for the changes found in the Folio text of *Lear* include several other appeals to various technical processes in the acting company. For example, it is proposed that some cuts in the Folio were made to reduce the casting requirements for a touring version.[19] This theory is suggested by the elimination of the Doctor in 4.7, and by occasional reductions in the numbers of servants needed. But any reduction in the players required to perform the script must take into account the practice of doubling some roles. Any practical economy in casting would require reducing the numbers of actors for the large scenes of pageantry and confrontation that involve all available members of the company.[20] Such reductions are found in the six "bad quarto" versions, which seem to have been adapted for casts of ten or twelve: 1594 *Contention* (*2 Henry VI*); 1595 *True Tragedy* (*3 Henry VI*); 1597 *Romeo and Juliet*; 1600 *Henry V*; 1602 *Merry Wives of Windsor*; and 1603 *Hamlet*.[21] Such is clearly not the case with the Folio text of *King Lear*, which cannot be performed with less than a full company of at least sixteen players.

Another suggestion is that the Folio text embodies changes made in the promptbook as a result of the experience the company had with actual performances before audiences.

Muir theorizes that the mad arraignment of Goneril and Regan in 3.6 was cut because the audiences laughed. It is hard to see why such a response would lead to cutting the passage, since many of the lines are purposefully and painfully witty. But a more serious objection must be raised. Revisions in *King Lear* frequently involve the addition of matter on themes of social justice or official iniquity. Others, by judicious cutting, point up the moral ambiguities or failings of men in high places. These themes apparently were considered sensitive by the censor.[22] Since the official promptbook was a legal entitlement to perform only the words which were approved in it, it seems unlikely that the book would be so altered after it had been licensed. As a practical consideration, the most convenient and economical time to make changes in a play script is before the preparation of the promptbook. After the book is made and approved, individual actors' parts must be copied out. Changes such as those found in *King Lear* involve complex passages of dialogue and would necessitate a recall and a painstaking revision of actors' parts at least, if not also a new submission of the book for approval by the censor.

Finally, there are positive indications that the script of *King Lear* as it appears in the Folio is Shakespeare's final version. The dramatic boldness, sensitivity, and power demonstrated by the variants in the Folio declare that only a masterful playwright is at work: the entrance of France, Burgundy, and Gloucester in the first scene; Edgar's exit from 1.2; Oswald's entrance at the end of 1.4; Goneril's entrance in 2.4; the details of plotting, staging, and characterization in the scene between Kent and the Gentleman, 3.1; the exit from 3.6, as Gloucester urges Kent to carry out the sleeping king; the exit after Gloucester's blinding and the associated changes in Edgar's speech at the transition from 3.7 to 4.1; the elimination of all of 4.3, effecting contextual changes in later scenes; the entrance of Cordelia's Gentleman to Lear, Edgar, and Gloucester in 4.6; the elimination of the Doctor in order to concentrate attention on Lear and Cordelia in 4.7; the exit of Lear and Cordelia at the end of 4.7; and finally the overall reordering of the character of Albany.

E. E. Stoll evokes the creative energy that may be felt when

Shakespeare's works and processes are approached with awe, wit, and excitement:

> And just because of the largeness of the undertaking, [Shakespeare] has necessarily had—for consistency of illusion, swiftness of movement, and intensity of effect—to contrive more audaciously and variously, and (in turn) to make such amends or adjustments as he could, sometimes even by artifices which are scarcely art. He evades and hedges, he manoevers and manipulates, he suppresses or obscures. But his most noble and effectual amends is positive—his poetry. The premise sets him free for it—*praecipitandus est liber spiritus*—and he walks not soberly afoot, like your philosopher, but flies.[23]

To discover the play disguised in the script, one must learn and apply the secrets of plotting, tempo, and movement in the theater. Careful comparison of the Quarto and the Folio texts of *King Lear* offers abundant lessons in Shakespeare's own style of enriching the performance of his plays: surprises, quickenings of rhythms, and the repeated endowment of movement with meaning.

There can be no absolute certainty as to the source of the variants in *King Lear*, but the different hypotheses may be tested against the evidence and against one another. R. S. Crane offers valuable guidance for the process of testing:

> The only proof there can be of a hypothesis about any particular thing lies in its power of completeness and coherence of explanation within the limits of the data it makes significant—and this always relatively to the other hypotheses pertinent to the same data with which it has been compared. We must be guided, however, in choosing among alternative hypotheses, by a further criterion—the classic criterion of economy: that that hypothesis is the best, all thing being equal, which requires the fewest supplementary hypotheses to make it work or which entails the least amount of explaining away.[24]

By every standard, the theory of Shakespearean revision as the basis for variants in *King Lear* offers a more powerful, more complete, and more coherent explanation for the data than any other theory so far stated. Every process envisioned in this theory is well within the observed performance range of the agents known to have influenced the text. No compositor is held responsible for brilliant strokes of stagecraft, no copyist is needed to have a rich supply of Shakespearean synonyms at the tip of his tongue, no bookkeeper is required to have acted suddenly in an innovative manner never before observed in bookkeepers. Instead, all that is needed is Shakespeare, capable of preternatural brilliance, well within his observed capacity to strike us dumb with amazement.

ABBREVIATIONS OF FREQUENTLY CITED WORKS

Chambers, *Facts and Problems* — E. K. Chambers, *William Shakespeare: A Study of Facts and Problems*, 2 vols. (Oxford, 1930)

Colie and Flahiff, eds., *Some Facets of "King Lear"* — Rosalie L. Colie and F. T. Flahiff, eds., *Some Facets of "King Lear": Essays in Prismatic Criticism* (Toronto, 1974)

Doran, *Text of "King Lear"* — Madeleine Doran, *The Text of "King Lear"* (Stanford, 1931)

Furness, ed., *New Variorum Edition* — Horace Howard Furness, ed., *King Lear, a New Variorum Edition* (1880; rpt. New York, 1963)

Greg, *First Folio* — W. W. Greg, *The Shakespeare First Folio: Its Bibliographical and Textual History* (Oxford, 1955)

King Lear, New [Cambridge] Shakespeare — George Ian Duthie and John Dover Wilson, eds., *King Lear*, The New [Cambridge] Shakespeare (Cambridge, 1960)

Muir, ed., *King Lear* — Kenneth Muir, ed., *King Lear*, The

	New Arden Edition, 8th ed., rev. (Cambridge, Mass., 1966)
The Riverside Shakespeare	G. Blakemore Evans, textual editor, *The Riverside Shakespeare* (Boston, 1974)

Notes

Chapter I

1. Unless otherwise noted, quotations from Shakespeare are taken from *The Norton Facsimile: The First Folio of Shakespeare*, ed. Charlton Hinman (New York, 1968), cited as "Folio." Through line numbers (TLN) from Hinman's facsimile and modern act, scene, and line numbers from *The Riverside Shakespeare*, textual ed. G. Blakemore Evans (Boston, 1974), are given. Thus the lines quoted here are cited: Folio, 398-403; 1.2.63-68. In all quotes, *u* and *v*, *i* and *j*, *s* and *f*, as well as typographic ligatures have been normalized according to modern conventions; turned-over or turned-under lines are regularized; italicized proper nouns in the dialogue of the original are here printed in roman type; and obvious errors such as turned or jumbled letters are silently corrected (for example, where the original reads "swear.st" I give "swear'st," and where the original has two succeeding speech-headings that read "*Lent.*" and "*Kear.*" I give "*Kent.*" and "*Lear.*").

2. The Quarto text is most readily available in *King Lear, 1608 (Pied Bull Quarto)*, Shakespeare Quarto Facsimiles, 1, ed. W. W. Greg (1939: rpt. Oxford, 1964). Quotations from this unpaged text will be given with page signatures followed by act, scene, and line numbers, again taken from the Riverside edition.

3. W. W. Greg, *The Shakespeare First Folio: Its Bibliographical and Textual History* (Oxford, 1955), p. 383, hereafter referred to as *First Folio*.

4. Charles Knight, ed., *The Pictorial Edition of the Works of Shakespeare*, 8 vols. (London, [1839-]1843), VI, 393.

5. Fredson Bowers, *On Editing Shakespeare* (Charlottesville, Va., 1966), p. 32.

6. Phillip Gaskell, *A New Introduction to Bibliography* (Oxford, 1972), p. 338.

7. Lewis Theobald, "Introduction," *The Works of Shakespeare: In Seven Volumes* . . . (1733[-34]), I, xxxvii-xxxviii; Alexander Schmidt, *Zur Textkritik des "King Lear"* (1879), translated and summarized in Horace Howard Furness, ed., *King Lear, a New Variorum Edition* (1880; rpt. New York, 1963), pp. 368-69 (hereafter, *New Variorum Edition*).

8. See George Ian Duthie, *Elizabethan Shorthand and the First*

Quarto of "King Lear" (Oxford, 1949), for the final disposition of the argument.

9. Greg, *First Folio*, pp. 381, 378; see also Alice Walker, *Textual Problems of the First Folio* (Cambridge, 1953), pp. 51-52 (hereafter, *Textual Problems*).

10. George Ian Duthie, "The Copy for *King Lear*, 1608 and 1623," George Ian Duthie and John Dover Wilson, eds., *King Lear*, The New [Cambridge] Shakespeare (Cambridge, 1960), p. 132 (hereafter, New [Cambridge] Shakespeare); Duthie's earlier theory was proposed in his edition, *Shakespeare's "King Lear"* (Oxford, 1949). See also Leo Kirschbaum, *The True Text of "King Lear"* (Baltimore, 1945), for a similar awkward hypothesis.

11. Walker, *Textual Problems*, pp. 37-67.

12. Michael J. Warren, "Quarto and Folio *King Lear* and the Interpretation of Albany and Edgar," in David Bevington and Jay L. Halio, eds., *Shakespeare: Pattern of Excelling Nature* (Newark, Del., 1978), pp. 95-97.

13. R.W.B. McKerrow, "The Elizabethan Printer and Dramatic Documents," *The Library*, 4th series, 12 (1931-32), 264.

14. E. K. Chambers, *William Shakespeare: A Study of Facts and Problems*, 2 vols. (Oxford, 1930), I, 98 (hereafter *Facts and Problems*).

15. Doran, "Elements in the Composition of *King Lear*," *Studies in Philology*, 30 (1933), 37-38, 58. This article amplifies her discussion of the same material in Doran, *The Text of "King Lear"* (Stanford, 1931), pp. 122-37. In his Yale Shakespeare edition of *King Lear* (New Haven, 1931), Tucker Brooke concurs with Doran: "It is unlikely that anyone but the poet himself would have produced a manuscript as disorderly as the one from which the Quarto was evidently printed" (p. 154). Also concurring with Doran about many aspects of the Quarto, Peter W. M. Blayney suggests "its copy was a much altered autograph manuscript containing the 'unpolished' but probably near-final text of a play differing in some important respects from the play as we know it" (quoted from the prospectus of *The Texts of "King Lear" and their Origins*, 2 vols. [Cambridge, forthcoming]).

16. Doran, review of Greg's *The Variants in the First Quarto of "King Lear,"* in *Review of English Studies*, 17 (1941), 474.

17. Doran, personal letter, dated 9 November 1976.

18. Doran, *The Text of "King Lear,"* pp. 21-38.

19. Philip Williams, "Two Problems in the Folio Text of *King Lear*," *Shakespeare Quarterly*, 4 (1953), 451-60.

20. Greg, *First Folio*, p. 383; Hinman, *The Printing and Proof-*

Reading of the First Folio of Shakespeare, 2 vols. (Oxford, 1963), II, 512.

21. One possible exception is found in the Folio at TLN 669 (1.4.140-55), where one of the few clumsy cuts in the Folio text appears.

22. Andrew S. Cairncross, "The Quarto and the Folio Text of *King Lear*," *Review of English Studies*, 6 (1955), 252-58, argues that parts of both the First and Second Quartos were used as copy. J. K. Walton, *The Quarto Copy for the First Folio of Shakespeare* (Dublin, 1971), rejects the possibility that any of the pages of the Second Quarto were used.

23. Editors and critics who have argued that Shakespeare was responsible for the major revisions in *Lear* include Samuel Johnson, *The Plays of William Shakespeare, in Eight Volumes* . . . (London, 1768) (see particularly VI, notes to 77, 79, 99, 148, 166); Charles Knight, ed., *The Pictorial Edition of the Works of Shakespeare*; Howard Staunton, ed. *The Works of Shakespeare*, 3 vols. (London, 1866); Richard Koppel, *Textkritische Studien über Richard III und King Lear* (Dresden, 1877), summarized and translated in Furness ed., *New Variorum Edition*, pp. 364-67; R. H. Cunnington, "The Revision of *King Lear*," *Modern Language Review*, 5 (1910), 445-53; W. D. Moriarty, "The Bearing on Dramatic Sequence of the Varia in *Richard III* and *King Lear*," *Modern Philology*, 10 (1912-13), 451-71; Doran, *The Text of "King Lear"*; Hardin Craig, *A New Look at Shakespeare's Quartos* (Stanford, 1961), pp. 10-17; E.A.J. Honigmann, *The Stability of Shakespeare's Text* (Lincoln, Neb., 1965) pp. 121-28, 151-71; and Michael J. Warren, "Quarto and Folio *King Lear* and the Interpretation of Albany and Edgar," in Bevington and Halio, eds., *Shakespeare: Pattern of Excelling Nature*.

CHAPTER II

1. J. L. Styan, *Shakespeare's Stagecraft* (Cambridge, 1967), p. 53; Thomas Kyd, *The Spanish Tragedy*, 4.3.1-4, from W. W. Greg, ed., *The Spanish Tragedy with Additions*, The Malone Society Reprints (Oxford, 1925), lines 2910-15.

2. See Sister Miriam Joseph, *Shakespeare's Use of the Arts of Language* (1947; rpt. New York, 1966), p. 245.

3. This point was made and illustrated by J. L. Styan, "Sight and Space: The Perception of Shakespeare on Stage and Screen," *Educational Theatre Journal*, 29 (1977), 18-28.

4. See, however, Bernard Beckerman, *Dynamics of Drama: Theory and Method of Analysis* (New York, 1970).

5. Andrew S. Cairncross, ed., *The First Part of King Henry VI*, The Arden Edition of the Works of William Shakespeare (London, 1962), p. 7; John Dover Wilson, ed., *The First Part of King Henry VI*, The New [Cambridge] Shakespeare (Cambridge, 1952), p. 102.

6. Quotations from the Second Quarto of *King Lear* are taken from *M. William Shake-speare's King Lear: The Second Quarto, 1608, A Facsimile*, ed. Charles Praetorius (London, 1885). This passage is found at I3ᵛ; 4.6.188.

7. See W. W. Greg, *The Variants in the First Quarto of 'King Lear': A Bibliographical and Critical Inquiry* (London, 1940), pp. 31-32.

8. George Lyman Kittredge, ed., *The Tragedy of King Lear* (Boston, 1937), and G. Blakemore Evans in *The Riverside Shakespeare* give the reading "Marry, your manhood mew!", treating "mew" as an imperative verb rather than as an interjection. Although this is more satisfactory, nevertheless the speech still appears as a completed utterance, and the figure of the interrupted speech is suppressed.

9. These promptbooks are all in the Folger Shakespeare Library, catalogued respectively as *Lear*, 27, 5, 19, and 23. In Charles H. Shattuck, *The Shakespeare Promptbooks: A Descriptive Catalogue* (Urbana, 1965), they are listed as *King Lear*, 20, 28, 36, and 63 (hereafter, *Descriptive Catalogue*).

10. Styan, *Shakespeare's Stagecraft*, p. 208.

11. Maynard Mack, "The Jacobean Shakespeare," in John Russell Brown and Bernard Harris, eds., *Jacobean Theatre*, Stratford-upon-Avon Studies, 1 (New York, 1967), p. 12.

12. Meagher, "Vanity, Lear's Feather, and the Pathology of Editorial Annotation," in Clifford Leech and J.M.R. Margeson, eds., *Shakespeare 1971*, Proceedings of the World Shakespeare Congress, Vancouver, August 1971 (Toronto, 1972), p. 249.

Chapter III

1. In fact, half of Cornwall's speeches set by the apprentice, Compositor E, who worked on this Folio page are headed *Cor*. He set *Cor*. fifteen times and *Corn*. fourteen. In contrast, Compositor B, the other man involved in setting *King Lear*, never set *Cor*. for Cornwall; on the pages he was responsible for we find *Corn*. twenty-five times and *Cornw*. once. G. Blakemore Evans, in *The Riverside Shakespeare*, remarks: "*Cor*. [in] F1 [is] possibly correct, if *Cor*. is an abbreviated form of Cornwall." But nevertheless he prints the Quarto reading, *Glou*., in his text. Jay Halio, in the Fountainwell Drama Texts edition of *King Lear* (Edinburgh, 1973) gives the speech shared by *Alb*. and

Cor. (TLN 176) to Albany and Cordelia, but following the Quarto as his copytext he gives the speech at TLN 204 to Gloucester.

2. Inappropriately sounded trumpets are also heard in the climactic scenes of *Hamlet* and *Coriolanus*. In both, the trumpets are heavily ironic: Claudius commands trumpets, cannon, and kettledrums to celebrate his good will toward Hamlet. In the Folio text the final trumpet sounds at the same moment that Claudius prepares a cup of poison and offers it to the prince (TLN 3571; 5.2.282-83). In the last scene of *Coriolanus*, Aufidius and "conspirators" listen to the offstage noises that signify the greetings being offered to Coriolanus:

> *Auf.* . . . . therefore shall he dye,
> And Ile renew me in his fall. But hearke.
> *Drummes and Trumpets sounds, with great*
> *showts of the people.*
> *1. Con[spirator].* Your Native Towne you enter'd like a Poste,
> And had no welcomes home, but he returnes
> Splitting the Ayre with noyse.
>
> [TLN 3703-9; 5.6.47-51]

The flourish announcing the entrance of Albany, Goneril, and Regan seems to be in a class with these. See also, Francis Ann Shirley, *Shakespeare's Use of Off-Stage Sounds* (Lincoln, Neb., 1963).

3. In *Pericles*, 3.2., the figure of Ceremon, as he revives Thaisa with fire and music, completely dominates the stage. But such domination might detract from the intricately figured words and movement given to Cordelia at this point in *Lear*. Like Edmund's captain in 5.3, this vivid minor role is diminished in the Folio.

4. Carol Dixon, "*King Lear* and the Popular Tradition: Dialectic of the Inversion Metaphor," a paper read at the Shakespeare Association of America meeting, Toronto, April 1978. This important study should be more widely known.

5. Muir, *Shakespeare's Sources*, 2nd ed. (London, 1961), pp. 165-66.

6. Granville-Barker, "*King Lear*," in *Prefaces to Shakespeare*, edited, with introductions, by M. St. Clare Byrne, 4 vols. (Princeton, 1963), II, 68-74.

7. Edgar's failure to reveal himself to Gloucester until the end of the play is a major difference between Shakespeare's story and that of the Paphlagonian king in Sidney's *Arcadia*. Any of Shakespeare's contemporaries who recognized the derivation of the subplot would themselves have been surprised by the change. See Sir Philip Sidney, *The Countesse of Pembroke's Arcadia* (1590; facs. ed., Kent, Ohio, 1970), Book II, Chapter 10, pp. 144-45.

8. An interesting suggestion about the scene-numbering of this act in the Folio is made by Greg. In modern editions, "F's 'Scena Tertia' becomes iv.iv, 'Scena Quarta' becomes iv.v, and 'Scena Quinta' becomes iv.vi. The modern iv.vii, however, is headed 'Scaena Septima' in F. This suggests that the division was not in the promptbook, but was introduced by the collator when preparing the copy for F. He apparently began by dividing Act iv in Q correctly into seven scenes, then deleted Scene iii since it was not in the promptbook, and corrected the numbering of iv-vi to agree, but overlooked Scene vii" (*First Folio*, p. 388, note E).

9. Alexander Pope, ed., *The Works of Shakespeare in Six Volumes, Collated and Corrected by the Former Editions by Mr. Pope* (1723-25; rpt. New York, 1969), III, 78n.

10. Kittredge, ed., *The Tragedy of King Lear*, p. 207.

11. Hereward T. Price, *Construction in Shakespeare*, University of Michigan Contributions in Modern Philology, no. 17 (Ann Arbor, 1951), p. 21.

Chapter IV

1. Concerning the use of rhymes to signal an exit, or as part of an interrupted exit, Warren D. Smith, *Shakespeare's Playhouse Practice: A Handbook* (Hanover, N.H., 1975), proposes that "the real reason Shakespeare's players required such obvious cues for their exits probably lies in a fact too often forgotten: his company played repertory. Unlike lines, exits are not memorized verbally. On the contrary, they must be coupled kinesthetically with lines, cues, and especially with stage groupings" (p. 99). Smith's point has also been made by critics discussing stage directions in the dialogue of medieval plays, where, it is suggested, playwrights had to consider that many of their actors might be illiterate and would have to learn their parts by ear.

2. A. C. Cawley, ed. "Secunda Pastorum," *The Wakefield Pageants in the Towneley Cycle* (Manchester, 1958), lines 569-74; or Martial Rose, ed. [and trans.], "The Second Shepherds' Play," *The Wakefield Mystery Plays* (Garden City, N.Y., 1962), p. 228.

3. Smith, *Shakespeare's Playhouse Practice*, pp. 104-5.

4. Though not marked in modern texts, staging practices of Shakespeare's theater would require Edgar to remove the body. There was no curtain to draw at the end of a scene. Corpses had to be carried off, in full view of the audience. Edgar says what he'll do with Oswald: "heere, in the sands / Thee Ile rake up, the poste unsanctified / Of murtherous Letchers." Then he has a rhyming

couplet, a usual signal for an exit, which he addresses to dead Oswald: "for him [Albany] 'tis well, / That of thy death, and businesse, I can tell." Capell, in his edition, added a stage direction reading: "Exit Edgar, dragging out the Body." Two gross improbabilities arise if this removal isn't managed here. First, since Edgar has to get Oswald out at the end of the scene, he'll be leading his blind father with one hand and tugging the corpse with the other. A very clumsy exit, at best. Second, Edgar's last speech in the scene, beginning "Give me your hand," becomes a totally uncharacteristic response by Edgar to his father's morose yearning for insanity. On other occasions in 4.6 and 5.2, Edgar encourages him and corrects Gloucester's gloominess whenever he hears it. Edgar's line becomes completely consistent and "in character," however, when we realize that he should not be onstage while Gloucester speaks.

5. A period is by no means an unusual punctuation mark at the end of a speech that is interrupted. Most modern editors use a dash here, indicating that the sentence breaks off abruptly.

6. This point was also made by Richard Koppel in the nineteenth century, but his argument, as well as Dr. Johnson's, is simply ignored in all recent discussions of the text (*Textkritische Studien über Richard III und King Lear*, p. 88, summarized and translated in Furness, ed., *New Variorum Edition*, p. 366). W. W. Greg independently comes to many of the same conclusions about the theatrical benefits of severely reducing in the Folio all questions about the role of France in the attempted rescue of Lear. But Greg nowhere in his discussion of this issue suggests who might have made the beneficial cuts. See "Time, Place, and Politics in *King Lear*," *Modern Language Review*, 35 (1940), 431-46; rpt. in *Collected Papers*, ed. J. C. Maxwell (Oxford, 1966), pp. 332-40.

7. The earliest extant promptbook of *King Lear*, from Dublin's Smock Alley in the 1670s, cuts from this speech a number of words and phrases, evidently in an effort to make it less tortuous:

Kent: . . . Albany, and Cornwall:
Who have, as who have not, ~~that their great Starres~~
Thron'd and ~~set~~ high; Servants, ~~who seeme no lesse,~~
Which are to France ~~the~~ Spies ~~and Speculations
Intelligent~~ of our State. . . .

The cancelled words are circled for cutting in the promptbook. This promptbook, listed in Shattuck's *Descriptive Catalogue* as *King Lear*, 1, may be seen at the Folger Library.

8. Zitner, "*King Lear* and Its Language," in Rosalie L. Colie and

F. T. Flahiff, eds., *Some Facets of "King Lear": Essays in Prismatic Criticism* (Toronto, 1974), p. 7.

9. Colie, "Reason and Need: *King Lear* and the 'Crisis' of the Aristocracy," in Colie and Flahiff, eds., *Some Facets of "King Lear,"* p. 192.

10. Emrys Jones, *Scenic Form in Shakespeare* (Oxford, 1971), p. 185; Walker, *Textual Problems*, pp. 51-52; Chambers, *Facts and Problems*, I, 238; Doran, *Text of "King Lear,"* pp. 73-75.

11. A suggestion for how the actors might move in the beginning of this scene appears at the opening of the chapter in Sidney's *Arcadia*, telling the story of the Paphlagonian king, source of the Gloucester subplot: "It was in the kingdome of Galacia, the season being (as in the depth of winter) very cold, and as then sodainely growne to so extreame and foule a storme, that never any winter (I thinke) brought foorth a fowler child: so that the Princes were even compelled by the haile, that the pride of the winde blew in their faces, to seeke some shrowding place with a certaine hollowe rocke offering it unto them, they made it their shield against the tempests furie" (Book II, Chapter 10). The actors playing Kent and the Gentleman might come together, and with cloaks extended towards one another shroud themselves against the storm while they speak. The different turns to move to an exit would be amplified visually when an actor closed his cape in preparation for turning to face the wind once again.

The relation of this play to pastoral conventions is discussed in Maynard Mack, *"King Lear" in Our Time* (Berkeley, 1965), p. 65, and Nancy R. Lindheim, *"King Lear* as Pastoral Tragedy," in Colie and Flahiff, eds., *Some Facets of "King Lear,"* pp. 169-84.

Chapter V

1. Two valuable discussions of "theatrical emblems" are Dieter Mehl, "Emblems in English Renaissance Drama," *Renaissance Drama*, n.s. 2 (1969), 39-57, and John Reibetantz, "Theatrical Emblems in *King Lear*," in Colie and Flahiff, eds., *Some Facets of "King Lear,"* pp. 39-58.

2. Sir Thomas Elyot, *The Boke Named the Governour* (1531; facsimile rpt. Menston, England, 1971), Book II, Chapter 13, fols. 162^v-63. Shakespeare's possible use of Elyot is discussed in Kenneth Muir, ed., *King Lear*, New Arden edition, p. 198, and at greater length by F. T. Flahiff, "Edgar: Once and Future King," in Colie and Flahiff, eds., *Some Facets of "King Lear,"* pp. 229-35.

3. Quoted in Curtis Brown Watson, *Shakespeare and the Renaissance Concept of Honor* (Princeton, 1960), p. 55.

4. *The True Chronicle Historie of King Leir*, in Geoffrey Bullough, ed., *Narrative and Dramatic Sources of Shakespeare* (New York, 1973), VII, 383-84; Scene 22, lines 1899-912.

5. Mack, " 'We Came Crying Hither': An Essay on Some Characteristics of *King Lear*," in Gerald W. Chapman, ed., *Essays on Shakespeare* (Princeton, 1965), p. 148.

6. For example, in "Player in Action: John Gielgud as 'King Lear,' " an unpublished study of Gielgud's 1940 production of *Lear*, Hallam Fordham reports: "Albany commences to read the letter. Edmund now enters hurriedly. . . . The contents of the letter give Albany complete ascendency over Edmund; he answers him superciliously, and walks away." (This typescript is in the Folger Library; it is listed in Shattuck's *Descriptive Catalogue* as *Lear*, 107.) The same interpretation was used in the 1975 New York Shakespeare Festival production, starring James Earl Jones.

7. See Carol Ann Heeschen Replogle, "Shakespeare's Use of the Forms of Address" (diss., Brandeis, 1967), a surprising and valuable study.

8. In contrast, Furness, ed., *New Variorum Edition*, gives a far more thorough analysis of nearly every major variant than is found in any recent text. Although great advances have been made in matters of textual analysis, modern bibliographers and editors show a shocking disregard for alternative opinions in cases where *literary* judgment must be applied. For example, Muir's three arguments against the Folio's speech-ascription here were convincingly refuted by Knight a century before. What distinguishes Furness's *New Variorum* from modern editions is his careful summation of viewpoints that he respects but must reject.

9. Felperin, *Shakespearean Romance* (Princeton, 1972), pp. 117-18.

10. The conventional gloss on this line was first proposed by Capell: "These words are made very intelligible by the action accompanying; the wide display of his hands, and the lifting up of his eye, both directed towards the heavens, would shew plain enough that it is they who are called upon to *fall*, and crush a world that is such a scene of calamity. . . . 'Fall, heaven! and let things cease!' " (quoted in Furness, ed., *New Variorum Edition*, p. 340). Furness offers a caveat unheeded and unrecorded by more recent editorial commentators: "Capell's interpretation may be the true one; and yet, an address to the Heavens, unaccompanied by any invocation, is unusual, to say the least." Furness also considers the simplest possibility: "If 'Fall and cease' be addressed to Lear, there is a curt harshness in the words which is scarcely in keeping with Albany's character." I submit that the "curt harshness" is in the words. Albany says them, and they cannot be easily explained away.

11. Madeleine Doran comments, "Albany's pious judgment is palpably false." *Endeavors of Art: A Study of Form in Elizabethan Drama* (Madison, Wisc., 1953), p. 334.

12. In one of the few negative responses to Albany, Walter C. Foreman, Jr., *The Music of the Close: The Final Scenes of Shakespeare's Tragedies* (Lexington, Ky., 1979) accurately describes Albany's "terrible incompetence as a leader" and his negligence leading to the deaths of Lear and Cordelia (pp. 144-50).

13. William R. Elton, *"King Lear" and the Gods* (San Marino, Cal., 1966), p. 298; Leo Kirschbaum, "Albany," *Shakespeare Survey*, 13 (1960), 30; Curtis Brown Watson, *Shakespeare and the Renaissance Concept of Honor*, p. 359; Peter Mortenson, "The Role of Albany," *Shakespeare Quarterly*, 13 (1965), 224.

14. Duncan S. Harris, "The End of *Lear* and a Shape for Shakespearean Tragedy," *Shakespeare Studies*, 9 (1976), 261.

15. William Frost, "Shakespeare's Rituals and the Opening of *King Lear*," *The Hudson Review*, 10 (1957-58), rpt. in Clifford Leech, ed., *Shakespeare: The Tragedies: A Collection of Critical Essays* (Chicago, 1965), pp. 199-200; Elton, *"King Lear" and the Gods*, p. 301.

Chapter VI

1. Sonneck, "The History of Music in America—A Few Suggestions," *Papers and Proceedings of the Music Teachers' National Association*, 11 (1916), 52. Sonneck was the first head of the Music Divison of the Library of Congress and the foremost bibliographer in the field of American music.

2. Much of Walker's thinking in her chapter on *King Lear* in *Textual Problems* seems to have been derived from Greg's earlier article, "The Function of Bibliography in Literary Criticism Illustrated in a Study of the Text of *King Lear*," *Neophilologus*, 18 (1933), 241-62; in turn, Greg's last statements on the *Lear* text, in *First Folio*, pp. 375-88, show that he accepted many of Walker's observations about the text, though he questions her reasoning and he does not subscribe to her conclusions.

3. W. W. Greg, "Special Transcript of the Three Pages," in Alfred W. Pollard, ed., *Shakespeare's Hand in "The Play of Sir Thomas More"* (Cambridge, 1923), pp. 228-29.

4. Wilson, "Bibliographical Links Between the Three Pages and the Good Quartos," in Pollard, ed., *Shakespeare's Hand*, p. 122; supplementing Wilson in the discussion of spelling, see Alfred W. Pollard, "Shakespeare's Text," in Harley Granville-Barker and G. B.

Harrison, eds., *A Companion to Shakespeare Studies* (Cambridge, 1934; rpt., Garden City, N.Y., 1960), p. 277; and E. Maunde Thompson, "The Handwriting of the Three Pages Attributed to Shakespeare Compared with His Signatures," in Pollard, ed., *Shakespeare's Hand*, p. 96.

5. The oddly spaced words here are noticed by Pollard in "Shakespeare's Text," cited above. However, they are transcribed as if they were completely regular (that is, without abnormal spacing) in all the transcripts of the Shakespearean pages in *Sir Thomas More* likely to be consulted by interested students. These include Greg's transcription in Pollard, ed., *Shakespeare's Hand*; Thomas Clayton's in *The "Shakespearean" Addition in the Booke of Sir Thomas Moore: Some Aids to Scholarly and Critical Shakespearean Studies*, Shakespeare Studies Monograph Series, 1 (Dubuque, 1969); and G. Blakemore Evans' in *The Riverside Shakespeare*.

6. See S. W. Reid, "Compositorial Spelling and Literal Rhyme: The Example of Jaggard's B," *The Library*, 5th series, 30 (1975), 108-15.

7. McKerrow, *An Introduction to Bibliography for Literary Students* (Oxford, 1929), p. 241; emphasis added. See further, Alfred W. Pollard, "Elizabethan Spelling as a Literary and Bibliographic Clue," *The Library*, 4th series, 4 (1923), 1-8.

8. Chambers, *Facts and Problems*, 1, 481.

9. Bowers, *On Editing Shakespeare*, p. 26.

10. Maxwell, "The Copy for *Timon of Athens*, 1623," in J. C. Maxwell, ed., *The Life of Timon of Athens*, The New [Cambridge] Shakespeare (Cambridge, 1957), p. 93.

11. Peter W. M. Blayney informs me in a letter of 16 January 1979 that "Okes's [the printer of the Quarto] type-supply led to a surprising amount of the Q mislineation. *Lear* was the first play-quarto ever printed by Okes or by his predecessors in the same business (founded 1598), and from it Okes learned that one can't print a play seriatim with 120 lbs. of type bought for printing prose pamphlets by formes." See his *Texts of "King Lear" and Their Origins*, forthcoming.

12. Alan E. Craven, "Simmes' Compositor A and Five Shakespeare Quartos," *Studies in Bibliography*, 26 (1973), 56. See also, Chambers, *Facts and Problems*, 1, 179-80, for further discussion of "memorial errors."

13. Greg similarly raises strong objections to the kinds of memorial error Walker proposes (*First Folio*, pp. 154-56). But in his discussion of the *Lear* text he questions her methods only in the most diplomatic terms.

14. In answer to my inquiry, Professor Doran wrote: "The quarto looked like an author's draft in bad shape which gave the compositors a bad time. . . . But there is reason for doubt, and it is there whether the passages are regarded as revisions or as first composition. They [the misaligned passages] imply that Shakespeare wrote out his verse as if it were prose, and at the same time did not worry about whether it would scan. Even if these passages *are* an overlay of revisions, they still mean that Shakespeare was content to compose his verse in this rough way. . . . I can't believe such a process in Shakespeare" (9 November 1976).

15. Greg, *First Folio*, p. 379; his position is stated at greater length in "The Function of Literary Criticism Illustrated in a Study of the Text of *King Lear*," in *Collected Papers*, ed. Maxwell; "I find it quite impossible to believe . . . that any writer, however familiar with the stage he might be, would in composition either deliberately or unconsciously introduce these features, which unnerve his language and destroy his verse, and then prune them away in revising the acting version" (p. 253). The "unnerving" and "destructive" features cited by Greg in this early article are in fact minor aberrations such as an extra syllable in a line or a superfluous qualifying phrase at the end of a long speech.

16. Duthie, "The Copy for *King Lear*, 1608 and 1623," in Duthie and Wilson, eds., *King Lear*, the New [Cambridge] Shakespeare, pp. 124-25. One revealing paradox in Duthie's analysis of the *Lear* text is his willingness to grant a remote possibility that Shakespeare did some theatrical cutting, but he sees no chance that Shakespeare changed or added after his initial composition: "There is no basis for any theory of a Shakespearean revision separating Q1 and F (apart from whatever share Shakespeare may have had in the work of abridgement)" (p. 124). Duthie seems to propose a kind of schizoid existence for the playwright. When he is away from the theater he writes but never erases, and when he is in the playhouse he joins the other actors in cutting, but "there is no basis" to think that he might change a word or add a line. See also, Richard Hosley, Richard Knowles, and Ruth McGugan, *Shakespeare Variorum Handbook: A Manual of Editorial Practice* (New York, 1971), which also fails to recognize the possibility, or the editorial consequences, of Shakespearean revision.

17. Muir, *Shakespeare's Sources*, pp. 165-66.

18. For a thorough discussion of the kinds of literary revision in Shakespeare's plays, see E.A.J. Honigmann, *The Stability of Shakespeare's Text*.

19. Duthie, "The Copy for *King Lear*, 1608 and 1623," p. 124.

20. William A. Ringler, Jr., "The Number of Actors in Shakespeare's Early Plays," in Gerald Eades Bentley, ed., *The Seventeenth-Century Stage: A Collection of Critical Essays* (Chicago, 1968), pp. 110-34, especially p. 123n.

21. See Robert Burkhart, *Shakespeare's Bad Quartos: Deliberate Abridgments Designed for Performance by a Reduced Cast* (The Hague, 1975).

22. Chambers, *Facts and Problems*, I, 98-117.

23. Elmer Edgar Stoll, *Art and Artifice in Shakespeare* (Cambridge, 1933; rpt. London, 1963), pp. 168-69.

24. Crane, *The Language of Criticism and the Structure of Poetry* (Toronto, 1953), p. 179.

Index

audience response, 47, 51-52; and expectations, 51, 66, 77-78; and interrupted exits, 56-57, 60, 62, 64-65, 79; and interrupted speeches, 19-20, 31; and textual variants, 37, 39-40, 49, 73, 87-88, 92-93

"bad quartos," 146
Beckerman, Bernard, 16, 20n
Blayney, Peter W. M., 10n, 136n
Bowers, Fredson, 5-6, 136, 142
Brooke, Tucker, 10n
Burkhart, Robert, 146n

Cairncross, Andrew S., 11n, 22
Capell, Edward, 66n, 71, 122
Cawley, A. C., 57n
censorship, 10, 77, 147
Chambers, E. K., 10n, 14, 77, 136, 137, 140-42, 147n
Clayton, Thomas, 132n
Colie, Rosalie L., 77
Craig, Hardin, 15n
Crane, R. S., 148
Craven, Alan E., 137n
Cunnington, R. H., 15n

delayed response, 37-38, 39-40, 113-14, 117-20
Dixon, Carol, 44n
Doran, Madeleine, 10-11, 15n, 77
dramatic necessity, 74, 114
dramatic texts, 17-18
Duthie, George Ian, 7, 8, 28, 80, 137, 143n, 146

Elton, William R., 127n
Elyot, Sir Thomas, 83
Evans, G. Blakemore, 4, 28, 28n, 39n, 132n, 144-46

Felperin, Howard, 121
Flahiff, F. T., 83n
Fordham, Hallam, 103n
Forman, Walter C., Jr., 127n
France, "invasion" of Britain, 67, 68, 71-74, 93-94, 97-98, 100
Frost, William, 127n
Furness, Horace Howard, 115n, 122n

Gaskell, Philip, 6
Gielgud, John, 103n
Granville-Barker, Harley, 48, 80
Greg, W. W., 4, 8, 10, 11, 12n, 27n, 53n, 72n, 130-40, 142

Halio, Jay, 39n
Harbage, Alfred, 28, 39, 80
Harris, Duncan S., 127n
Hinman, Charlton, 12-13
Honigmann, E.A.J., 15n, 143n
Hosley, Richard, 143n

interrupted action, 31-33
interrupted exit, 42-43, 56-71
interrupted speech, 18-33, 43-44, 46, 70

Johnson, Samuel, 15n, 72
Jones, Emrys, 77

King Leir, the True Chronicle Historie of, 91-92, 135
Kirschbaum, Leo, 127n
Kittredge, George Lyman, 28, 28n, 53n
Knight, Charles, 4, 15n
Knowles, Richard, 143n
Koppel, Richard, 15n, 72n
Kyd, Thomas, 16

Lindheim, Nancy R., 77n

McGugan, Ruth, 143n
Mack, Maynard, 34, 77n
McKerrow, R.W.B., 9-10, 11
Macready, William Charles, 32
Maxwell, J. C., 136
Meagher, John C., 34
Mehl, Dieter, 82n
Moriarty, W. D., 15n
Mortenson, Peter, 83, 127n
Muir, Kenneth, 28, 47-48, 71, 80, 83n, 114-15, 146-47

Pollard, Alfred W., 132n
Pope, Alexander, 53
Price, Hereward T., 54-55
promptbook(s), 6, 13, 32, 145
pronouns of address, 111-13

Reibetantz, John, 82n
Reid, S. W., 134n
Replogle, Carol Ann Heeschen, 111n
rhyme, 56-57, 60-63, 66n, 134
Ringler, William A., Jr., 146n
Roberts, James B., 32
Rose, Martial, 57n
Rowe, Nicholas, 33

Schmidt, Alexander, 7
Second Shepherds' Play, 57
Shakespeare, William
  as director, 16
  As You Like It, 35
  Coriolanus, 41n
  Hamlet, 41, 142; Second Quarto of, 10, 131, 132, 140-43
  2 Henry IV, 142
  1 Henry VI, 22
  3 Henry VI, 21-22
  Julius Caesar, 102
  King John, 113
  King Lear
    First Quarto, sources of copy for, 6-11, 129-36, 139-40
    Second Quarto, 11; compositorial editing in, 23-25
    Folio, sources of copy for, 12-15, 17, 140-49
    modern composite text, basis of, 3-9, 129; problems introduced by, 17, 20-22, 25-26, 28-29, 37-38, 40-42, 50, 52-53, 70-71, 79, 111-16
    theatrical revision, 13-15, 23-26, 32, 36-42, 46-55, 144-46
  Macbeth, 69
  Othello, 141, 142
  Pericles, 41n
  Richard II, 137
  Sir Thomas More, 130, 132, 135, 140, 141-42
  Timon of Athens, 136, 140, 143
  Troilus and Cressida, 56-57, 141, 142, 143
Shirley, Francis Ann, 41n
Sidney, Sir Philip, 42n, 77n, 86
Smith, Warren D., 57
Sonneck, Oscar George Theodore, 129
spectacle, 40-42
speech headings, 36-40, 113, 131
Staunton, Howard, 15n
Stoll, Elmer Edgar, 147-48
Styan, J. L., 16, 33

Theobald, Lewis, 4, 7
Thompson, E. Maunde, 132n

Wakefield Master, 57
Walker, Alice, 4, 8-9, 77, 130-40
Walton, J. K., 11n
Warren, Michael J., 9, 15n
Watson, Curtis Brown, 127n
Williams, Philip, 11n
Wilson, John Dover, 22, 132

Zitner, Sheldon P., 176

PRINCETON ESSAYS IN LITERATURE

The Orbit of Thomas Mann. By Erich Kahler

On Four Modern Humanists: Hofmannsthal, Gundolf, Curtius, Kantorowicz. Edited by Arthur R. Evans, Jr.

Flaubert and Joyce: The Rite of Fiction. By Richard Cross

A Stage for Poets: Studies in the Theatre of Hugo and Musset. By Charles Affron

Hofmannsthal's Novel "Andreas." By David H. Miles

Kazantzakis and the Linguistic Revolution in Greek Literature. By Peter Bien

Modern Greek Writers. Edited by Edmund Keeley and Peter Bien

On Gide's Prométhée: Private Myth and Public Mystification. By Kurt Weinberg

The Inner Theatre of Recent French Poetry. By Mary Ann Caws

Wallace Stevens and the Symbolist Imagination. By Michel Benamou

Cervantes' Christian Romance: A Study of "Persiles y Sigismunda." By Alban K. Forcione

The Prison-House of Language: a Critical Account of Structuralism and Formalism. By Frederic Jameson

Ezra Pound and the Troubadour Tradition. By Stuart Y. McDougal

Wallace Stevens: Imagination and Faith. By Adalaide K. Morris

On the Art of Medieval Arabic Literature. By Andras Hamori

The Poetic World of Boris Pasternak. By Olga Hughes

The Aesthetics of Gyorgy Lukács. By Béla Királyfalvi

The Echoing Wood of Theodore Roethke. By Jenijoy La Belle

Achilles' Choice: Examples of Modern Tragedy. By David Lenson

The Figure of Faust in Valéry and Goethe. By Kurt Weinberg

The Situation of Poetry: Contemporary Poetry and Its Traditions. By Robert Pinsky

The Symbolic Imagination: Coleridge and the Romantic Tradition. By J. Robert Barth, S. J.

Adventures in the Deeps of the Mind: The Cuchulain Cycle of W. B. Yeats. By Barton R. Friedman

Shakespearean Representation: Mimesis and Modernity in Elizabethan Tragedy. By Howard Felperin

René Char: The Myth and the Poem. By James R. Lawler

Six French Poets of Our Time: A Critical and Historical Study. By Robert W. Greene

Coleridge's Metaphors of Being. By Edward Kessler

The Lost Center and Other Essays in Greek Poetry. By Zissimos Lorenzatos

Shakespeare's Revision of "King Lear." By Steven Urkowitz

Library of Congress Cataloging in Publication Data

Urkowitz, Steven, 1941-
    Shakespeare's revision of King Lear.

    Includes bibliographical references and index.
    1. Shakespeare, William, 1564-1616. King Lear.
2. Shakespeare, William, 1564-1616—Criticism, Textual.
3. Shakespeare, William, 1564-1616—Stage history—To 1625.
I. Title.
PR2819.U7   822.3'3   79-3234
ISBN 0-691-06432-6

Lightning Source UK Ltd.
Milton Keynes UK
UKOW06f1036070217
293807UK00002B/123/P